MY ISRAEL EXPERIENCE

A Memoir

YONATAN SHAKED

Copyright © 2021 by Yonatan Shaked

All rights reserved. No part of this book may be used or reproduced in any manner whatsoever without written permission, except in the case of brief quotations embodied in critical articles and reviews. Please direct all inquiries to the author by email at johnnyshaked@gmail.com

Book design by Yonatan Shaked

Author's Note: I have not changed the names of individuals or places in this book but occasionally have omitted names to maintain their anonymity. I have written an honest account of my life in Israel but also recognize that the memories and events I describe in this book may differ from those of certain individuals mentioned or not mentioned by name. It is not my intention to hurt any individual but only to tell my story and my truth.

ISBN: 979-8-7041-0317-2

Chapter 1
My Introduction to Israel

In 1967 my name was John Robert Screeton, but then I went to Israel and it changed my life. It was just after the Six Day War when I travelled by train from Paddington Station to France, and from there I sailed to Israel. After I disembarked from the ship at the port of Haifa I took the bus to Tiberias.

The bus was unlike anything I had seen in England and looked more like a truck. It was square with small windows and the seating was not upholstered. Strewn along the narrow aisle were woven straw baskets packed with fresh herbs, garlics and root vegetables. I found a place to sit, next to a man wiping the sweat with a dirty rag from his dark and wrinkled brow. As I sat down on the hard wooden seat and had placed my little suitcase upon my lap, I was struck by the strong body odour that oozed from the pores of his skin. I was curious and turned to take a look at the sunburnt man, but I quickly turned away again. I became intrigued by these oriental Jews, by their dark skins, by the women's colourful headscarves and the men's yarmulkes and black curly sidelocks.

It was stifling hot on the bus and the passengers were fanning themselves from the intense heat, or was it the stench of excrement and wet feathers? There were wire cages filled with live chickens, and I began to feel queasy. Someone opened a window and suddenly the fresh air came rushing in; the sights and smells were unusual, but now I inhaled the sweet perfume of orange blossom.

As the bus made its bumpy descent towards Tiberias, I looked out of a small window to the green orchards and fertile land beyond, but then the scene suddenly changed; a great blue lake was spread out before me, filling my entire view with indigo. My heart beat quickly when I realised that I was looking at the Sea of Galilee, and my mind was cast back to the pictures in my Christian Bible of Jesus and the miraculous catch of fish. As the bus came closer to the lake, the local fishermen could be seen on the shore with their fishing nets, and for a moment I was sure that it was Jesus and his disciples.

In Tiberias I transferred to another bus which took me to Kibbutz Ein Gev on the eastern shore of the Sea of Galilee.

As I descended the bus at Kibbutz Ein Gev, the first thing that struck me was the pungent smell that came from the cowsheds. I was wearing a grubby, khaki coloured safari jacket, carrying my suitcase in one hand, and in the other hand a letter of introduction from the Kibbutz Volunteers Office. But the next thing that struck me was the Golan Heights towering above me; reports of Syrian artillery shells raining down on Kibbutz Ein Gev came to mind. But then I heard a voice calling: "Volunteers over here!"

It came from the house mother who supervised the volunteers. She was a robust woman, in her early fifties, with a ruddy complexion and a perpetual beaming smile. She read my letter of introduction and studied me with a grin.

"My name iz Pnina," she said, in Austrian accented English. "*Yihr* name ist Johnny in zer kibbutz!"

She then she let out a great laugh and took me by the arm to her office where she registered my details in her book.

Pnina handed me one woolen blanket, some sheets, and a set of kibbutz work clothes in the uniform blue colour, and then she showed me to my room which I would be sharing with two other volunteers. My bed was a sturdy metal frame with a straw mattress. I threw my supplies down onto the mattress and breathed a sigh of relief to have finally made it to my destination.

Work started each morning at five-o-clock in the banana plantation. The pale complexion that I had when I arrived changed quickly to a healthy tan, my fair hair became bleached by the sun, and I developed a healthy physique from physical work and wholesome kibbutz food. In the evenings I went to disco parties organised by the volunteers. We danced the Twist and in the course of the evening the lights were turned down and we danced in couples to French ballads, swaying back and forth, closely knit together, in a slow-dance routine. Eventually, we wandered down to the lakeside with our partners and found a quiet spot to make love.

I adapted quite well to my new way of life with the mainly non-Jewish volunteers, but I learnt about the Jews from kibbutz members, many of whom had blue numbers tattooed on their arms from the concentration camps.

The kibbutz members were Jews, but they kept none of the Jewish tradition other than Israeli national holidays: there was not even a synagogue on the kibbutz, it being a kibbutz which followed a Marxist ideology. One of the veteran kibbutz members, named Gesia, invited me to her home to meet her family, but I was shy and did not possess conversation skills, and when she held my hand I almost shied away. My own mother had never held my hand and where I came from there were many secrets; I knew nothing about my own mother, so when Gesia told me stories about her life I felt that she was telling me her darkest secrets. She told me how her first husband was killed defending the kibbutz in the War of Independence leaving her pregnant, and with a six year old daughter. I was dumbfounded and did not pursue the subject, but when she told me how she came to Eretz Yisrael — Palestine — illegally, and how her family had remained in Russia and were murdered by the Nazis, I was speechless.

Gesia told me many stories about kibbutz life, describing to me their socialist lifestyle upon which the kibbutz ideology is based: working for their keep and without pay.

"Johnny, we are communists!" she joked.

Indeed, I learnt from Gesia how everything was communal in the kibbutz. There was a communal dining room where everybody ate together, the food was cooked in the communal kitchen by members assigned to kitchen work, and the laundry and ironing was done in the communal laundry. Gesia told me that in the beginning the members shared the same clothes – even the same underwear – and received a change only once a week, whereupon they sometimes ended up with shirts that were too short or for others that were too long. In the communal sewing house kibbutz members made clothes from canvas tents, and the maternity dresses were made from the same English suit fabric bought in bulk. Her stories warmed my heart.

Gesia belonged to a group who had come to British Mandate Palestine before World War II from Latvia in Russia, and who founded Kibbutz Ein Gev on the eastern shore of the Sea of Galilee – south of the border from the French Mandate of Syria – in 1937. She re-married a fisherman named Mendel and gave birth to a third daughter. Mendel went on to become an authority on the Sea of Galilee and wrote books about the fishermen in the New Testament, about their fishing methods, and about the ancient harbours around the Lake. Many of the tourists who came to hear Mendel's lectures thought that he was a Christian because of the immense knowledge he had of the Christian Bible.

Gesia and Mendel became my adopted family for the duration of my stay on Kibbutz Ein Gev. When I expressed a wish to stay on in the kibbutz, Mendel arranged me private lodgings in a splendid location. My new room had a lawn outside with a large Eucalyptus tree, and I had a magnificent view of the Sea of Galilee. I was in Paradise.

Gesia was a handsome woman, and there was something very agreeable in how she carried herself which I observed every evening when she walked into the kibbutz communal dining room. After a hard day's work and a shower, her salt-and-pepper hair was oiled and glistening, and her facial skin was creamed and glowing. Gesia wore smart cotton dresses that she had sewn, and she always looked noble in appearance. Once in a while, however, the barber came to the kibbutz to give a haircut to all the kibbutz members, and when I saw Gesia with a short-back-and-sides haircut nothing could have shocked me more!

The emphasis on the kibbutz was hard work, however, that had not occurred to me when I was judging them by their looks; but these women – whom I had judged so harshly – were holocaust survivors with numbers tattooed on their arms.

One of them was a lady named Ilana. She was always laughing and she had every good reason to laugh: her only child, who was in the Israeli Navy and had been sent to Portsmouth, England, to join the submarine crew aboard the INS Dakar, was sailing home to Israel. I observed her happiness, but I looked at the blue number tattooed on her arm and tried to comprehend what she must have suffered in a concentration camp in Nazi Europe. And yet, here she was, living a new life on a kibbutz in Israel.

Ilana worked in the communal dining room, and she radiated the joy of a proud mother while pushing the yoghurt trolley from table to table. Her big eyes, however, were somehow sad looking. She had strong defined facial features with high cheekbones, her hair was jet black, cropped like the other women on the kibbutz, and as she pushed the trolley she always spoke cheerfully about her son. One day, when stopping at a table and ladling out the yoghurt, in all her excitement she knocked the full bucket of yogurt over. It crashed onto the stone floor, splashing the fermented creamy substance all over the diners, but she roared with laughter.

A few days later I saw Ilana supported on both sides by kibbutz members after hearing the news that all contact with the INS Dakar and its crew had been lost. (Eventually all the crew members were declared dead, and the INS Dakar was not found for more than thirty years.) Her face was dreadful to look at, the colour had drained to a pale yellow, her eyes were staring out from their dark sockets, and she snarled like an angry animal. To see this woman's tragedy and to imagine her pain after all that she had suffered in the concentration camps was inconceivable to me.

I did not know how to express my sadness, but I went down to the lake so that I could be alone, and cry alone. I had a secret spot by the lake where I went from time to time, and I treasured those moments when alone. The Sea of Galilee was serene and mirror-like, and I was able to watch the fishing boats and fishermen working in the dusky distance. It reminded of the pictures in my Christian Bible, except that from my secret spot by the lake those pictures had come to life.

Chapter 2
Are you a Jew?

The road to Kibbutz Ein Gev is lined with eucalyptus trees, and beyond are fields of date palms. After a short stint working in the banana plantation I then worked a whole year in date cultivation, experiencing the tradition of offshoot propagation in which I helped prepare the offshoots that grow from the trunk of the female palm. I planted them in the fields behind those eucalyptus trees.

Pollination was done in the early springtime when we took the flowers from within the sheath of a male tree and collected the pollen to pollinate the female flowers. Work also included irrigation, and finally we did the harvesting using a forklift to reach the dates. I would then drive the red Massey Ferguson tractor with a full load of dates on the trailer, singing all the way to the central packing house on the southern tip of the Sea of Galilee.

I was into my second year on the kibbutz when it was suggested that I become a member of Kibbutz Ein Gev. If I decided to, it would be put to the vote in a manner that everything was decided on the kibbutz. Certainly I had settled in nicely, and at this point in time I had an Israeli girlfriend. It was therefore recommended that I change my status from tourist to that of citizen, under the Law of Return.

The Law of Return is a law that gives Jews the right to return and settle in their ancestral homeland.

For the process of becoming a citizen I was sent by the kibbutz to the Ministry of Interior in Tiberias. There I filled out the necessary forms stating that I was Jewish. I was not lying: I *believed* that I was a Jew. Indeed, it was a strange phenomenon. Ever since I can remember, there was something that pulled me to the Jews and that was why, when the Six Day War broke out, I volunteered to go to Israel.

I was suntanned and blond, sitting in front of a clerk who was a dark-skinned Yemenite Jew - with a twinkle in his black eyes. He looked deeply into my blue eyes, and asked: "Are you a Jew?"

I was momentarily stunned by the question, but I stared back into his black eyes and told him what I wanted to believe: I told him that I have a Jewish mother. I also told him that I planned to marry my Israeli girlfriend and settle down on the kibbutz. He stamped the documentation and I was made a permanent resident.

I was then issued a *Laissez-Passer* for a three year period before I could become a fully-fledged Israeli citizen, on the basis of being Jewish.

In the meantime I was affiliated with the volunteers and joined them on familiarization trips around Israel that were arranged by our tour guide, a friendly *kibbutznik* named Arieh. He also happened to be the kibbutz landscape gardener and indeed was a lover of nature. Arieh sincerely enjoyed taking the volunteers around the country in typical kibbutz fashion, travelling by truck with a supply of canned food such as sweet corn and meatloaf, and staying in youth hostels and Christian hospices.

But tragedy struck in the summer of 1969 when Arieh was killed doing his reserve duty on the Suez Canal. It was a dreadful shock for all us volunteers, and the first time that a friend had fallen in action.

I was living a Jewish façade, going through the motions of life from behind a veil and yet, as my façade became intertwined with the happy and tragic events of life on the kibbutz, so did my façade begin to be my identity.

Around this time I left my job in date cultivation and started a new job on the kibbutz dairy farm.

The dairy farm had a staff made up of volunteers, kibbutz members, and Israel Defence Forces' personnel serving in the *Nahal*.

Nahal is the Hebrew acronym for *Noar Halutzi Lohem*, meaning "Fighting Pioneer Youth", a group who did their military service combined with work on an agricultural settlement.

Work on the dairy farm included milking with automated milking machines, feeding, calving and general work around the farm. Socially life was better because we dairy farmers were a sort of *clique* who ate together in the communal dining room, and due to the odd working hours we had special privileges. For example, after the evening milking we had sausage, sour cream and *halva* — which may sound trivial, but they were delicacies on the kibbutz.

In the evenings, my newly acquired friends came to lie down on the lawn under the Eucalyptus tree. We drank tea together and listened to Tchaikovsky and Beethoven, and when my limited supply of gramophone records ran out, we just lay gazing up at the stars in the quiet of the night.

I had many responsibilities on the farm and grew to love the fragrance of sweet smelling hay, fresh alfalfa, and the sharp tang of fermenting silage. One morning I was sent with a soldier from the *Nahal* to transport bales of hay from the haystacks to the sheds. The bales of hay weighed more than forty kilograms each, but we worked hard and with vigour. We pulled the bales out from the bottom tier, the top bales toppled down, and we stacked them onto the trailer. We did this to a rhythm: pull-drop-stack, pull-drop-stack, but it was difficult to keep the tempo up; the bales from the top tier tumbled onto us and we laughed so much. We threw our exhausted bodies onto the hay and lay there in silence.

But then the soldier held my hand.

It was not uncommon for men to hold hands in the Levant but nevertheless it was new to me. We lay there chatting in the hay, while holding hands, but something stirred within me. I could feel the blood running through my veins. I turned to look at him and was just admiring his curly black hair and upturned nose burnt from the sun, when suddenly he jumped up and we continued our work.

The next morning he did not come to work and I was told that his army unit had left for manoeuvres.

The weeks passed, but his memory clung to me like a sickness. I went for walks down to my private spot by the lake, but now with a feeling of melancholy. The weather was cooler and the lake was like a pond, and reflected in the lake was the city of Tiberias. At first there was not a sound, but then there was a slight stirring in the lake, a ripple on the surface, a sudden gust of wind, and a violent storm blew up. The waves plunged to the shore and I stood up, singing at the top of my voice to the wild sea. I felt ecstatic, but then the *Sharkia* storm ended and all became calm once again.

My room on the kibbutz was divided with a bamboo partition, and behind the partition I had my bed. I covered the lampshades with red bandannas to diffuse the glare of electric light bulbs, and I painted the furniture in various shades of green. One evening I was reading on my bed behind the partition when there was a knock at the door.

"Come in," I called out.

Only when he came behind the partition did I realize that it was the soldier and my heart gave a small tremor. He sat down on my bed and took my hand in his, squeezing it tightly. He told me in a solemn voice where he had been in the army.

"Johnny," he said in a hurry; "I want you to come to my parents for the Passover festival."

I did not know when Passover was – or *what* Passover was – but I said that I would like to very much.

Then there was another knock at the door, and a boisterous Dutch volunteer barged in. She saw the soldier sitting on my bed with his hand in mine, and she stood there with her eyes wide open.

"Hmm, *what's* going on here?" she growled.

The soldier was caught red-handed and ran away.

Chapter 3
My first Passover

On the eve of Passover I took a crowded bus to the village in central Israel where the soldier and his family resided. They lived in a small but cosy bungalow that reminded me of England. It had a well-kept garden with magnolia trees, and a pomegranate tree next to the front gate.

I was warmly received by both parents but immediately led into the kitchen by the mother. The kitchen table was covered in a red and white Gingham-check oilcloth, and the room was filled with the aromas of roasting meat and chicken broth.

Sara, the soldier's mother, was a short lady with dark hair, olive skin and a tired look; she had dark shadows under her eyes from weeks of preparations and pre-Passover cleaning. She served me a bowl of borscht soup and busied herself in the kitchen while asking me about my parents, what they do, where they are from, and why they do not come to Israel.

She served me another ladle of borscht, and while she was preparing the Passover meal, she told me stories of how she came from Poland to Palestine before World War II, and about her family who were murdered by the Nazis. As I ate my soup I watched her attending to the different pots simmering on the gas rings, taking a taste of this and a taste of that, and I noticed that she had a small upturned nose, exactly like her son the soldier. When I finished my borscht soup she took me to the soldier's bedroom to show me where I would sleep, handed me a stiffly-starched towel, and showed me to the shower.

After I had showered and rested, Sara entered the bedroom and placed a cup of Turkish coffee next to my bed. She told me to get ready for synagogue and informed me that her son the soldier had not come home. I was less concerned about him not coming home than I was about going to a synagogue; I had never set foot in a synagogue before. She gave me a yarmulke and I hurried off to synagogue with Yoel, the soldier's father, not knowing what to expect.

We sat in the second row of the mahogany-wood pews, and I was reminded of a church. I was astonished to see the flaking walls and amateurishly painted murals of pitiful looking Holy Land scenes, but what struck me more were the Eastern European, peasant-looking, religious congregants; they were nothing like the people I knew on Kibbutz Ein Gev who were intellectual and secular. Nevertheless, as the service started, I stood in prayer with my yarmulke securely clipped onto my head, and I prayed as a Jew prays.

Yoel was a farmer, a rugged man with a strong grip, and one of the first settlers in the village. After the service we walked back to the house and he practiced his English with stories about his life in Mandatory Palestine, where he was born. As we entered the house I gave a sigh of relief when I saw the soldier's uniform, army boots, and Uzi machine gun strewn over the stone floor, with the comforting sound of running water in the shower.

Yoel and Sara were beaming with joy as the other guests arrived and took their places at the large dining table, elegantly laid for the traditional Passover *Seder*. The vibrant emerald-green dining room walls were stencilled in a cream coloured diamond design, the amber glass chandelier tinted the room a sunny yellow, and once we were all seated we proceeded with the ritual of retelling the story of the Exodus from Egypt. The recital of the *Haggadah* took many hours, songs were sung, and we ate unleavened bread with four cups of wine.

After the festivities the soldier suggested that we go for a walk so that he could smoke a cigarette, but upon leaving the house I noticed that he took with him a bunch of keys. As we strolled down the street I admired the quaint little houses and their lush gardens; all of them filled with exotic shrubs and trees with sweet-scented blossoms. The night air was fresh and I inhaled a deep breath as we entered the garden of a vacant house.

The soldier unlocked the door to the vacant house but the air inside was stifling hot, and it was pitch-black. I was reminded of the ten plagues that we had just read about, but I followed him through the darkness into a room where he lit a candle and opened the wooden shutters. The flame flickered in the dark, and I watched ghost-like shadows jumping on the walls. We got undressed in candle-light and climbed onto a single bed.

The following day we slept late and at noon his father made *Kiddush* – the sanctification of the holiday – and we ate another festive meal. In conversation, the soldier told me that he would like to visit England after his military service and suggested that we meet there.

After sundown I took the bus back to Tiberias and dozed for much of the journey with thoughts of my experience with the soldier. My mind was set on returning to England, and yet I was due to become a member of Kibbutz Ein Gev. But there was nothing I could do about it; I was infatuated. The following morning I informed Mendel, my adopted father, that I was leaving the kibbutz. He expressed his deep sorrow but arranged for the kibbutz to pay my passage home to England, and as soon as I had a sailing date I left the kibbutz.

For my remaining days in Israel I stayed with the soldier and his family in central Israel. He had already purchased a flight ticket but I sailed from the port of Haifa. From the deck I watched the glorious Bahai Shrine with its magnificent terraced gardens disappearing into the Israeli shore-line, and I was left with happy memories. But then a shudder of fear went through me: I was returning home to my past I had erased.

Chapter 4
Yom Kippur War

While in England I rented a room in Golders Green, a Jewish neighbourhood. I got a position with El Al, Israel's national airline, at Heathrow airport, but my sole aim was to return to Israel.

I stayed for three years in England, and in those three years I had relationships with men. I also had a circumcision, because it is written *every male among you shall be circumcised*, and by the time that I returned to Israel I identified as gay Jew. Consequently, I did not consider the possibility of returning to Kibbutz Ein Gev and the people I loved so dearly. As a gay man, life on a kibbutz would have been out of the question. Instead, I headed for Tel Aviv.

I got a position with TWA at Lod Airport but on the eve of Yom Kippur, on Friday, 5 October 1973, I finished my shift and took the bus to Yoel and Sara's house, to be with them for the fast.

The Sabbath is a day of rest in Israel when public transport ceases and the shops are closed. However, on Yom Kippur, the Sabbath of Sabbaths, the country comes to a complete standstill; there is no transportation, no radio, and no television broadcasts.

I had fasted before on Yom Kippur but on this particular Yom Kippur I fasted *and* went to synagogue. I was standing in prayer for the Afternoon Service, at a time when the air in synagogue was stifling hot and the sour bodily smells rose up from the sweating congregants. The fans blew but they did not cool. The foul-smelling breath of a congregant reciting prayers wafted over. Suddenly there was a commotion in the synagogue and the congregants stopped praying. They closed their prayer books and turned to talk to one another, discussing why some congregants were being led out of the synagogue. I turned to Yoel to ask what was happening, but he was praying and could not be disturbed. Then I saw his youngest son being led out, but Yoel continued to pray — now with added fervour.

The worshippers commenced with the Concluding Service, and the synagogue became completely silent as the ark was opened for all to see. I stood there, looking at the Torah Scrolls, not knowing what to expect next.

The congregation cried aloud:

We have acted treasonably, aggressively and slanderously;
We have acted brazenly, viciously and fraudulently;
We have acted willfully, scornfully and obstinately;
We have acted perniciously, disdainfully and erratically.

I listened in awe to the words and continued reading from my prayer book:

Turning away from thy good precepts and laws has not profited us. Thou art just in all that has come upon us; thou hast dealt truthfully, but we have acted wickedly.

We have acted wickedly and transgressed, hence we have not been saved. O inspire us to abandon the path of evil, and hasten our salvation, as it is written by thy prophet: Let the wicked man give up his ways, and the evil man his designs; let him turn back to the Lord who will have pity on him, to our God who pardons abundantly.

The words seemed to speak to me and my conscience was pricked.

The ark was closed and there was a rush to finish the service. Something was very wrong, but I still did not know what.

At the end of the service the ram's horn was sounded and the congregation shouted out loud:

Next year in Jerusalem!

But then came the Evening Service, and we stood in silent prayer once again.

Yoel would not talk to me as we hurried back to the house; he was extremely anxious. When we arrived home, the radio was on broadcasting the call-up codes — and both his sons had been taken away already. I sat down with Yoel and Sara at the bare table listening to the radio broadcasts, but the news bulletins were constantly interrupted with special call-up codes: all civilian reserves were being called to duty.

Israel had been invaded by the surrounding Arab countries in a surprise attack, on the holiest day of the year, and we were unprepared. A blackout was imposed and the sirens started to wail.

Sara got up to turn the lights off, and she prepared coffee and cake to break the fast. Neither of them spoke as they listened to the call-up codes and news bulletins, but then Sara turned to me and said assertively:

"Johnny, you'll stay here with us, you can't go home. It's war."

It took three days to mobilize Israel's civilian reserves but in the meantime Egypt had succeeded in crossing the Suez Canal, and Syria had advanced into the Golan Heights. Yoel went to synagogue every day, Sara hurried to the grocery store to bring supplies, and all I could do was pray for the boys and the safety of Israel. We listened to the news on the radio all the time.

The Soviet Union mounted a massive sea and airlift to re-supply the Egyptian and Syrian armies, and then there was a decision by the United States of America to mount a massive airlift to Israel. Lod Airport had been closed because there were no civilian aircraft, but now I was called in to the airport to help with offloading the massive airlift as it arrived.

The fighting lasted for almost three weeks in which time, in the south, Israel managed to capture parts of Sinai, trapping the Egyptian army; in the north, Israel had advanced to just twenty two miles from Damascus, the capital of Syria. On the home front we heard nothing from the boys, and for weeks after the war we still did not know whether they were dead or alive.

We lived in complete silence. At nighttime I cried when thinking of Yoel and Sara in their pain. The waiting for news was unbearable and it crossed my mind that it was harder on the home-front than in battle. I had begun to imagine the worse. So many soldiers were already lost and somehow it did not seem likely that they would ever come home.

But when they did eventually come home, they were in no mood for rejoicing. They told me horrific stories of how the enemy had tortured and killed Israeli soldiers, and of how the Syrians had mutilated the corpses.

After the war I returned to Tel Aviv, but I found a different city. The people were angry and there was murkiness in the air. The war had been a psychological blow to the Israeli population, and as the number of casualties became clear they directed their anger towards those in the government.

I went about my daily chores but any joy I had when returning to work was only dampened upon hearing of those who had lost their loved ones.

The casualties went up, there were border incidents after the ceasefire, and it never seemed to end.

Israelis, however, are an optimistic people and, as painful as the war had been, life got back on track and the coffeehouses and restaurants began to fill up once again. I came home from work one day and a letter awaited me. It was from the Israel Defence Forces informing me that since applying for citizenship when on the kibbutz, I had accumulated three years in Israel and would be drafted for my compulsory army service. I would have to leave my job, leave my apartment, and I would not receive a salary.

It was as if the director of the movie had called "cut!"

Chapter 5
Army Service

Military service in Israel is mandatory and as a rule Israelis are called-up at the age of eighteen for a three-year service. I was with a group of relatively older, new-immigrant soldiers drafted for a special fifteen month service to be trained in the Israeli Artillery Corps.

The first days were spent standing in line getting our kit-bag, uniform, boots and identity tags while getting our vaccination shots at the same time. They also took photographs, checked our blood type, and finally gave everyone a short-back-and-sides haircut.

We were sent to do our basic training in the hills, three miles north of Jerusalem in the West Bank. In the army we referred to the area as *Yosh*, which is the Hebrew acronym for *Yehuda VeShomron*, which is Judea and Samaria. The base was next to an unfinished royal palace that was in the process of being built before the Six-Day war by the Hashemite Kingdom of Jordan.

It was a severely cold and wet winter, and I was very much looking forward to the heated living quarters in a clean military building with lockers and rows of beds in perfect alignment. To my utter dismay, we were put in a row of tents in a remote corner of the base which was bogged down in mud. The tents were vaguely visible in the grey fog that hovered over the hills, and when we finally arrived we discovered that inside each tent were four metal beds, sunken in the mud. On each metal bed was a rubber mattress covered in olive-green plastic.

Importance was given to marching, standing-in-formation, and the making of a military bed with perfect corners; and upon the military bed, the backpack, ammunition belt, and helmet were positioned for the morning drill. However, the tough, old canvas backpacks, and the ammunition belts, were so warped that they were impossible to smooth out. Our uniforms were dirty, our boots were caked in mud, and nobody passed the morning drills.

The various drills were physically demanding; we did push-ups, sit-ups, squad drill, stretcher drill, running, and more running. When we came back to base they would send us out again, and we would return soaked from perspiration. The wet uniforms were hung in the tent to dry while we slept, but when we got up at half past four for the morning drill, the uniforms had frozen on the lines. We had to wear our dirty uniforms and foul-smelling socks, and stuff our kit-bags with the frozen uniforms.

Then our first leave was due.

I had made arrangements to stay in the seaside resort of Netanya, in the central district of Israel. While on leave, I found some cardboard and cut it to fit the backpack and ammunition belt, squaring the edges to perfection. I cleaned my boots and took a supply of plastic bags to protect them from the mud when on the base before the morning drill. I laundered and ironed my uniform, then folded it and packed everything into plastic bags to keep it all neatly pressed.

Upon returning to the base, while at the standing-in-formation drill, the drill sergeant was impressed by my perfect appearance. At the military bed inspection, all the drill sergeants gathered around my bed – the one with the perfectly squared backpack and ammunition belt – and they had a discussion.

I was immediately promoted to Trainee Duty Officer and given the important assignments to do; it was my responsibility to set a good example and have the soldiers ready for all the drills. As a result, I gained the respect of the entire unit.

After completing four months of basic training we graduated and were then transferred to Shivta, the main Artillery Corps training base in the Negev Desert, in the south of Israel. On the first day I was sent to wash dishes for the entire base.

I had never seen so many dishes in my entire life; the endless dishes were piled high, and I thought to myself, "I didn't join the army to wash dishes!"

I felt that it was a total waste of time, and it broke me; I was playing the tough and able soldier, but it was not me. I was playing a role, but I could not play it anymore. I turned to the soldier washing dishes with me, and said: "I wish I could run away!"

He answered: "Me too! *Let's do it!*"

So we planned our escape.

Back in our sleeping quarters, when the other soldiers were fast asleep, we packed and locked up our kit-bags. We slept a few hours with our boots on, but when the time came for us to leave the other soldiers began to stir. They saw that we had arranged our beds and had placed our kit-bags neatly in place, and they were surprised that we were leaving. We told them that we had received special leave, and then we hurried to the main gate with our weapons.

But we did not have a pass to get out of the base, so we intentionally laughed and joked as we approached the gate, flashing a piece of paper in the hope that they would not check. I knew that the guards would not check me, the Trainee Duty Officer, and indeed they let us both through the barrier, wishing us a happy leave.

We were ecstatic but we had committed a serious crime: we had deserted and were now fugitives on the run! Each time an army vehicle approached we threw ourselves onto the sand dunes and lay flat until it passed. We continued doing this for the five kilometre stretch from Shivta to the main road, and from there we hitch-hiked to Beersheba.

Then we went our separate ways.

I went in the direction of Tel Aviv to visit a boyfriend. I called him from a telephone booth when I got to Tel Aviv, but I had not anticipated the angry reaction I got when I told him that I had run away. He refused to see me.

I had not understood the graveness of what I did. In fact, my boyfriend told me that I would go to jail and so, he agreed to see me on the condition that he would take me in the morning to the city military officer in Tel Aviv to give myself up. And so I agreed.

When I met the military officer I told him that I was a homosexual. His advice to me was frank and to the point. He said: "*Be a man!*" I told him that I was a man. Nevertheless, he referred me to the army mental health clinic. My army profile was dropped from 98 to 21 making me permanently unfit for military service and I was discharged from the army.

In civilian life in Israel, one was evaluated according to one's army profile when getting a job — and in society in general. Something was considered very wrong with you if you did not go to the army.

It is said that a person cannot change until he knows his own flaws. Indeed, I returned from my failed military service with the faint awareness that something was not quite right with me.

I rented a rooftop apartment in Tel Aviv on a quiet street, just off a boulevard leading down to the Mediterranean Sea, and I could smell the sea from my rooftop apartment. At night, when alone in my bed, I heard the sounds of elephants and other exotic animals that came from the nearby zoo.

I then started a new job in a travel agency. It was customary for shops in Tel Aviv to close for the *siesta* in the hot Israeli climate, and so for my daily *siesta* break I went to the beach to sit on the breakwater and have a picnic. While alone on the breakwater I stripped to sunbathe in my underwear. I listened to the meditative sound of waves playing against the rocks beneath me, and I would fall asleep to the enticing sounds. When I awoke I sat up and watched the dazzling sparkle that came from the midday sun reflecting like silver sequins upon the water. These mid-week *siesta* breaks were quite a contrast compared to the social gatherings that I went to on weekends, when everyone converged onto the Tel Aviv gay beach. It was a cruising ground for gay men searching for a sex partner. I met someone there and not only did we have sex, but we became lovers and settled down in a relationship together.

Chapter 6
Conversion to Judaism

In Tel Aviv I did not have God, and I did not have my Jewish identity anymore. Somehow my gay lifestyle had taken over. I confessed to my new boyfriend that I was not really a Jew, and he suggested that I convert to Judaism. I welcomed his advice but neither of us could have imagined the immense effect that conversion would have on the both of us.

Before approaching the Jerusalem Rabbinate I read books on Judaism and was spellbound by what I read. It awoke in me a yearning for a better life, and when I read about how it was to *be* a Jew, it seemed that one ascended to a higher realm when living a Jewish way of life. I knew that I had to be a religious Jew.

But when the time came to meet the rabbi in charge of conversions, I did not expect him to be so rude. I had read that they discourage would-be converts, but he was insensitive and accused me of wanting to have sex with Jewish girls. In fact, he told me to get out of his office. I returned, however, a second and a third time, and finally I was enrolled in a class for conversion.

The course was not a course about Judaism but rather about how to be a Jew. According to the Jerusalem Rabbinate, a Jew must be observant and committed to an Orthodox religious way of life.

Judaism dictates to you how to behave from the moment you get up in the morning until the time you go to sleep at night. It's a religion of deeds, of 613 commandments, and one is obligated to conduct oneself accordingly.

They told me to wear a yarmulke. Initially I was reluctant, but wearing a yarmulke actually did something to me; it acted as a reminder how *not* to behave. My yarmulke became a constant reminder that homosexuality is an abomination, and I accepted that. My boyfriend, however, had a frown on his face when I told him of the changes that I must make. He was stunned that I was taking religion seriously, and his face fell.

"You're leaving me aren't you?" he queried, as tears filled his eyes.

It was true. Nothing was more important to me than becoming a *real* Jew; I was filled with pride and was not concerned about his feelings. I cherished the opportunity to study Judaism, to learn the intricate blessings, and to know how to pray — the Jewish way. I learnt how to observe the Sabbath and how to keep a kosher home, and I even studied the elaborate laws appertaining to the slaughtering of an ox and the koshering of it.

Occasionally *Rebbetzin* Goren, the wife of Israel's Chief Rabbi, came to the class to test us orally. Upon hearing that I was British, the *rebbetzin* asked me a question.

"What is the blessing you would say upon seeing the Queen of England?" she asked.

"Blessed art Thou, O Lord our God, King of the Universe, whose strength and might fill the world," I answered, proudly.

However, I had recited the blessing that is said upon hearing thunder, and the *rebbetzin* corrected me, reciting the correct blessing upon seeing a king or queen:

"Blessed art Thou, O Lord our God, King of the Universe, who has given of thy glory to flesh and blood."

There are many different blessings for various occasions, and they should be recited accordingly. Throughout all of my life I always prayed to God but now the way to God was based on deeds, reciting blessings, and saying the set prayers. The emphasis in Judaism is not on Faith in God but rather it is a commitment in behaviour. Therefore, I cut all connections with my friends in Tel Aviv, and I started to live a Jewish way of life.

It troubled me, however, that with all the changes I was making, I was still exempt from the army.

I asked for a re-evaluation of my status and army profile, and after numerous interviews my army profile was raised again, and I was recruited back into the Israel Defence Forces. I had to do my basic training all over again, and thereafter I was called up every year for a month's reserve duty.

After the study period with the Jerusalem Rabbinate, and after more than a year of waiting, I was finally called in for my conversion.

I underwent a symbolic circumcision, where a single drop of blood was drawn, and then the immersion in the *mikveh* – a ritual bath – as the final rite of conversion. In the *mikveh* I affirmed that I intended to accept the yoke of the commandments, and then I officially became part of the Jewish people.

A convert to Judaism is no longer considered the son of his biological parents but is the son of Abraham and Sara. I took a new name – Yonatan – and also officially changed my surname to Shaked at the Ministry of Interior.

I could now be counted in a quorum for prayer services and so, on my first Sabbath in synagogue as a *real* Jew, I was called-up to recite the blessings on the Torah scroll with my newly adopted Hebrew name. This meant using my new name with *son of* Abraham. I was called-up for my *Aliyah* as: Yonatan ben Abraham

(Yonatan, son of Abraham), and then the rabbi and the congregants congratulated me with *mazal tov!*

At the end of the service, just as the women began emerging from behind the partition that separates men and women in prayer, the *rebbetzin,* the wife of the synagogue's rabbi, came to wish me *mazal tov!* I sensed, however, that she was being more friendly than usual.

"Yonatan," she said, addressing me tenderly with my new name; "have *I* got a girl for you!"

Before I could even grasp her words she pushed me behind the partition, into the women's section, where the girl was sitting with a beaming smile, ready and waiting for her match made in Heaven.

She was a very nice Jewish girl from a good family, plump and nothing outstanding to look at. The point was, I was already acquainted with her and her family, and I was very angry that no one had spoken to me about it.

I sat down and told the young lady of my plans. I told her that I had resigned from my job in Tel Aviv, and that I intended to move to Jerusalem to study in a *Yeshiva* – a rabbinical college. I also made it clear that I had no intention of getting married at that stage, and neither had it been my intention to go on dates while studying. I then watched the beaming smile drain from her large round face. And the *rebbetzin* never forgave me.

"You're making the mistake of your life," she said, in a huff; "and you'll never have such a chance again."

The *rebbetzin's* words echoed in my head. I had converted because I wanted a new life; indeed, I wanted to marry and to have children – but I had a problem. For that past year I had prayed with all my heart and with all my soul to *change*, but I knew that I was still a homosexual. I was using Judaism as a tool to suppress my feelings and to overcome my homosexuality by praying harder and by strict observance. I was still not ready, and for that reason I had to enter a *Yeshiva* to study Torah all day. I was convinced that if I study more about Jewish Law, and together with the practical application of the 613 commandments that dictate to a Jew how to live his life, it would purify me and keep me from anything defiling as homosexuality. I had to live a strict, religious way of life.

In the Yeshiva there is an accepted dress code of dark trousers, a white shirt worn over a small prayer shawl with fringes on the four corners, black shoes and a black yarmulke. I dressed accordingly and like most of the students I also grew a beard. I ate and slept at the Yeshiva like the other students. All of the students were expected to attend morning prayers at half past seven in the *Beit Midrash,* the study hall, where Talmud studies also took place.

There is a certain smell when one enters the *Beit Midrash*, of stale clothes and volumes of holy books, unique to *Yeshivas.* When I entered the *Beit Midrash* for early morning prayers there was also the distinct smell of fart. I thought that, when standing before God and uttering the holy words, it would have been inexcusable to fart. I saw it as an abomination, and all the more so while wearing *Tefillin*, the small black leather boxes containing scrolls of parchment with holy verses from the Bible. But I was wrong. The students farted and even the rabbis farted out loud.

The daily schedule was prayers, breakfast, Talmud studies, lunch, afternoon prayers, more Talmud studies, Jewish Law studies, Jewish ethics studies, dinner, more studies and finally the evening prayers.

I observed the commandments which the Torah places upon a Jew, and I took upon myself the Jewish way of life: a life based on deeds. I was now a real Jew and no longer had to pretend. But then, one morning I could not get out of bed due to a severe pain in my lower back. The hospital diagnosed it as a "fatigue fracture" which seemed strange because I had been sitting in the *Yeshiva* all day long. But when the doctor asked if perhaps I was under some sort of emotional stress, I broke down crying.

The Jewish way of life was not a natural way of life for me. It was forced and sometimes I felt that I was going against the grain. The changes had been too much for me to endure; it was as if something was telling me to *stop!* The doctor concluded that I probably had the fracture since childhood but emotional stress was causing the pain now. He put me in a full plaster body-cast and instructed me to lay flat for as long as it would take. A family in Jerusalem volunteered to take care of me until I was able to walk again.

Chapter 7
Jerusalem

Converting to Judaism and becoming a Jew meant that I had to repent and atone for my sins. Consequently the whole process created a change of consciousness in me. I thought differently and behaved differently and therefore, after a year in the *Yeshiva*, I returned to the real world a different person.

In the process of conversion I had rid myself of the past, but the soul given to me by God, my true essence, was suppressed. It was Judaism that controlled and dictated to me how to live, and in spite of everything it was not a natural way of life for me. Moreover, I fought my homosexuality by avoiding it and not practicing it, but the process of repentance did not make things right: I did not become a heterosexual.

I lived in a government building-project for singles in one of the new Jewish suburbs built around Jerusalem after the Six-Day war. East Talpiot was built on what was No Man's Land before the 1967 war, in an area between the Hashemite Kingdom of Jordan and Israel. My small apartment was within walking distance of the Old City, which enabled me to walk to the Western Wall on the Sabbath. I enjoyed walking and occasionally walked through the

Arab suburbs, making friends along the way; I went with love in my heart and was greeted by Muslim families, some of whom I have remained friends with until today.

When I wandered the hills and valleys around Jerusalem, I was moved to tears. I would walk through the hills, along the narrow tracks made by flocks of sheep, past caper bushes that grew from the cracks of ancient walls, while admiring their white flowers; the petals were very slightly washed in pink, and the graceful violet-coloured stamens swayed to and fro — like underwater sea anemones in an ocean current. Little buttercups lined the wayside, their radiant yellow-colour were like tiny lamps — put there to show me the way.

As I continued on I noticed a lull as the civilized world gradually became muffled by the surrounding hills. I was approaching the Arab village of Silwan with an element of excitement: walking over to the other side to where Jews do not roam. I looked up, and suddenly appearing out of nowhere the massive lead dome of the Al-Aqsa Mosque soared above me. I was stunned by the vastness of the mosque and had not expected to see it while wandering the hill-sides in the quiet of nature. I therefore retraced my tracks until I found an isolated spot, out of the presence of the imposing mosque, and sat down on the grass in a cross-legged position.

The scent of a mandrake plant intrigued me; the perfume of the yellow fruit was enticing but in the distance I saw two boys approaching on horses. As they trotted past, one called out "Shalom!" and the other, I noticed, kept his eyes set on me as they continued on their way. But then, just as I was contemplating whether to take the fruit of the mandrake, my heart stopped. The ground began to tremble from the thunder of hooves. I looked up and saw one of the boys galloping back towards me, and I stiffened with fear. He jumped off his horse and landed beside me.

The Arab boy had a strong physique and was wearing short trousers, which showed his muscular legs. He took a tight grip of my arm, and his body, held close to mine, radiated an intense heat with an odour of horses and sweat. He had come to inform me that the plant was poisonous, and then he released my arm but still remained very close. I inhaled his animal smell while studying his sun burnt skin and beautiful chestnut brown hair that fell into his penetrating green eyes. But without a further word he mounted his horse and galloped off towards Silwan.

On my walks I would often sit under the shade of a tree and admire the view of the Old City. I studied the golden beauty of the Dome of the Rock shrine, so large and magnificent, and felt inspiration. But I also observed the Al-Aqsa Mosque, standing gallant and upright with its solemn lead dome, and began to feel a strange uneasiness. I noticed that both the Dome of the Rock shrine and the Al-Aqsa Mosque were built upon the Temple Mount, and beneath them was the Western Wall — but a remnant of the Holy Temple. As the sun set I watched in awe as Jerusalem was decorated in gold. I closed my eyes, but when I opened them again it was twilight time. The obscure shapes of Jerusalem began to disappear into neutral shadows, punctuated by dots of yellow street lamps. As dusk fell I tried to understand God, the maker of such beauty, and religion, the cause of so much hatred.

I decided to purchase a box of watercolour paints and returned to the same place to paint my feelings on paper. The many hours that I spent painting the view, over and over again, embedded in me every dramatic detail of the landscape; so deeply was it impressed upon my soul that it became an intimate part of me. I painted a detailed vision, but I was unable to capture on paper the passion that I felt.

The apartment building where I lived had a somewhat whimsical atmosphere for the simple reason that all the tenants were singles. In those days I was inclined to be more sociable, and therefore I frequently teamed up with other religious singles to eat the traditional Sabbath meal. When I prayed in the various synagogues in and around East Talpiot I became acquainted with the congregants and was regularly invited to their homes to eat the Sabbat meal.

I discovered that there was a divide between the religious and secular citizens of Israel and it seemed, now I was religious that I belonged to an exclusive club. Indeed, I had this in mind when I started to look for work: I decided to look for a travel agency run by religious Jews, and I was fortunate to find a travel agency that was run by Hasidic Jews.

The small and hectic office was in an ultra-Orthodox neighbourhood with a mostly Hasidic clientele. They clambered over the crowded desks to get from one clerk to the next, frantically purchasing airline tickets and paying in cash with American dollars, in a totally different work atmosphere than I had ever been accustomed to working in before. They were noisy and ill-mannered, and when I complained to the manager about their rudeness, he replied, "Manners are for *goyim*!"

No receipts were given but rather a hand shake and a Yiddish "*mazel und broche*" said in jest to seal the deal, as one would do in the diamond trade. If they did not possess a passport they travelled on someone else's passport, for they all looked alike and dressed in Hasidic garb. They wore long black frock coats and black hats and they all had beards. Their white skin was often blotchy with eczema and many of them were overweight with large plump faces. In general their appearance was very unpleasant. And yet, I wanted to belong and tried *not* to look too nice by growing a full beard myself, and I wore greying white shirts, and a small prayer shawl underneath my shirt with the ritual fringes hanging outside: *that ye may look upon it, and remember all the commandments of the Lord, and do them; and that ye go not about after your own heart and your own eyes, after which ye use to go astray.*

The staff worked long hours, including Friday mornings before the Sabbath. The ultra-Orthodox women, who normally came frumpily dressed in dreary colours on weekdays, but would be travelling before the Sabbath, came to work already dressed in their Sabbath attire. I was startled to see one of them wearing an ostentatious fake satin gown in a lustrous purple colour, a bouffant styled wig especially for the Sabbath, and highly made-up. I chuckled when I saw the same lady on the Sunday after the Sabbath, who had travelled back in the morning, now looking completely dishevelled in the same gown and wig, but now reeking of body odour. I ventured to ask one of the ultra-Orthodox women how she takes care of her wigs and was told that the wigs are nylon and she simply throws them into the washing machine with the rest of her dirty laundry.

I had a friendly relationship with the proprietors of the travel agency, but I was a novelty for them because I was a convert. This apparently was the only reason they were nice to me, because they repeatedly told me that in the Torah they are *commanded* to love the proselyte. They also told me that I could never marry a girl from their community *because* I was a convert — unless she was tainted.

Nevertheless, I saw them as pious Jews as they claimed to be. Hasidic Judaism focuses on spirituality and mysticism with the emphasis on the Divine presence in everything, no matter how mundane. Therefore, it warmed my heart when I was invited to stay at their home for the Sabbath.

The ultra-Orthodox neighbourhoods were like self-imposed ghettos; a world of concrete and brick buildings built closely together, without trees, without flowers, and without any greenery. The only colour was the children's bicycles and plastic toys that hung over the ledges of small verandas. The streets were crowded with men in black hats, black suits and black frock coats, and women in layers of dull coloured clothing, long sleeves, black stockings and wigs – and some with black hats worn on top of the wigs. The birth rate was high and when I looked at these plump women I was reminded of a mother duck with feathers of grey, brown and black, waddling along with her many ducklings following.

In the household where I was invited, the walls were stark white with one large black-and-white picture on the wall, framed in heavy gilt, of an old rabbi who was their *Rebbe* – the leader – to whom they turned for advice on all matters. The heavy wood table, surrounded by solid wood chairs, was covered with a white tablecloth and covered once again in transparent plastic that reflected the bright lights above. Against one wall a highly lacquered wood bookshelf was filled with Talmud and other sacred books. These were the comforts of a Hassidic home: there was no sofa, no easy chairs, and no curtains.

Indeed, their customs were very different than I was familiar with. I watched in amazement when my host stood at the head of the table to recite *Kiddush* — the sanctification of the Sabbath. His large figure, clad in a long, shiny black satin jacket and a massive black fur hat, was dramatic under the bright lights, set against the stark white backdrop. It seemed more like a satire on Hasidim.

When we sat down to eat, we were served by his young wife who wore an exquisitely made French-style gown, adapted especially for Ultra-Orthodox women, and stunning high-heeled shoes which matched her manicured red fingernails and lipstick. Ironically, she conveyed a glimpse of the real world: she *appeared* completely secular, but her head was covered with a luxurious wig made of human hair.

Jewish Law requires a married woman to cover her hair but it was impossible to tell because her wig looked so real, except that in the duration of one evening she changed it from a long haired style to a short cut style. She also changed her fashionable clothes a number of times and by the end of the evening I was feeling quite dizzy.

When I was preparing to go to bed my host asked me to undress under the blankets so as not to offend God. In the morning I had to get dressed under the blankets, without washing, and so by the end of the Sabbath, when it was sundown, I was very much looking forward to going home.

My host, however, had other plans: my expertise was needed in the office and I had to work. The office was extremely full, but what seemed strange to me was that the Hasidic clientele were still dressed in their Sabbath finery of shiny satin frock coats, trousers tucked into their socks, and massive black fur hats — in the very small travel agency.

After a year working with them I found myself in a serious predicament. I was instructed by them to forge dates on airline tickets to undercut the fares, and when it was prayer time they insisted, in a moral act of righteousness, that I take a break to pray with them. This was an exceedingly long ordeal due to their deep concentration as they reached heights of spiritual pleasure by focusing on every single word in the prayer book.

I did not reach heights of spiritual pleasure! My soul was tormented by their conduct and I began to have a crisis. I honestly had thought that I was entering a better world, but instead I felt shame and disappointment. These Jews represented Judaism, but instead of being righteous they were corrupt. The words in the Bible resounded in my head:

You shall be to Me a kingdom of priests and a holy nation.

I plucked up the courage to ask my boss how it was possible that they cheat. He did not seem one bit offended by my brashness and claimed that he understood my dilemma. He justified their actions by saying that in Europe the Jews had been persecuted and were forbidden to work in many fields, and therefore they had to find ways to survive and it remained their way of life until this day.

I did not accept his answer and handed in my resignation. He gave me a severance package and wished me luck in finding another place of employment.

Chapter 8
The Old City of Jerusalem

In my quest to find a place in the world of Judaism, I joined a class for Torah studies in the Old City of Jerusalem which was led by a young and quietly spoken Modern Orthodox rabbi. He was exceptional insofar as he brought into his teaching sources from the *Kabbalah* and Jewish mysticism. He also taught meditation based on a practice known as *hitbodedut* – seclusion with God – which was the method taught by Rabbi Nachman, the founder of the Breslov Hasidic movement.

To get to his house in the Jewish Quarter, I entered the Old City by way of the Zion Gate and walked through the Armenian Quarter. As I walked along the narrow cobbled alleyways, my footsteps echoed loudly against the walls that soared high on both sides. I continued walking but heard an eerie whisper coming up from the cobbled path. I finally worked it out: it was the Armenians speaking behind tiny windows that lay flush with the cobbled pathway, and their muffled voices were bouncing off the cobblestones. Behind the thick walls I caught a glimpse of a fascinating culture that lived on the other side.

The rabbi greeted his students while sitting cross-legged, enwrapped in a prayer shawl, and wearing a brightly coloured yarmulke. After all of us were sitting cross-legged, he started the class with teachings about prayer and joy, and through him I learnt another side of Hasidic Judaism. He also taught us how to meditate on the Hebrew name of God, using the Hebrew letters *Yud-Hei-Vav-Hei*, but unlike other meditation techniques that I had previously learnt for relaxation and the calming of the mind, in this meditation we were required to take an honest look at ourselves in order to break down the barriers of denial, and enter the place of Truth. The meditation was so powerful that it shook me; the Truth was dangerous territory for me. Nevertheless, I continued going to class and enjoyed being in the company of people seeking a better spiritual life.

Occasionally, after class, I would walk down to the Western Wall to pray and went by way of the Arab *souk* while enjoying the spiritual heights of meditation. Along the way I inhaled the warm fragrances of freshly baked pita bread that came from the hot clay ovens, and occasionally I stopped at a stall to buy a round, toasted sesame bread with a small packet of *za'atar* – a mixture of hyssop with sesame seeds and salt. I continue down the crowded marketplace where Arab boys manoeuvred their brightly coloured carts packed high with supplies. I passed embroidered Bedouin dresses, *Keffiyeh* scarves, and colourful materials with sequins and coins which were hung on the outside walls. I continued on past the sugary scent of sweet shops, and the sharp bouquet of herbs that came from spices piled high in perfect pyramid shapes.

There was a *nargileh* coffee-house where men sat on raffia stools, smoking water pipes with sweet perfumed, fruit-flavoured tobaccos, and next door a shop with the strong aroma of freshly grounded Arabic coffee and cardamom. I purchased a blend of coffee to the noisy sound of grinding machines and continued down the steps, passing colourful hand painted Jerusalem pottery, and Hebron hand-blown glass in colours of greens and blues. I passed the dreadful smell of raw meat that hung outside the butcher shop, where swarms of flies accumulated under the glare of one bare electric light bulb, and then I found myself walking behind an *Imam* and inadvertently followed him as he entered the Chain Gate. I watched him ascend the Temple Mount and disappear into a fascinating world.

I did not feel a spiritual uplifting when at the Western Wall but I did feel an uncanny attraction to the place. I stepped back to take in a panoramic view of the area and tried to imagine it in the time of the First Temple: in my mind I pictured the Tabernacle with the Holy of Holies and the Ark of the Covenant where the presence of God dwelt since the time of the Exodus from Egypt.

Standing from afar with the Western Wall before me – the wall that surrounded the Second Temple – I then looked up at the imposing Dome of the Rock where the Foundation Stone is enshrined by the Muslims, and I recalled my meditation class with the rabbi. We learnt to enter the place *within us*, where God dwells, to the place of Truth: *to our own Foundation Stone.*

Looking up at the Dome of the Rock, I was mystified as to why so much importance was given to a place. I dwelt on that thought while eating my toasted sesame bread with *za'atar*.

I had been attending meditation class regularly but started to feel less enthusiastic about it; it was as if my Foundation Stone was causing turbulence as I came closer to the Truth. And then something strange happened to me as I was walking to class. An Armenian man looked at me, and as he caught my eye I felt a familiar feeling coming back again; a feeling that I had to deny. Up until then I had been fighting it by depriving myself of love and of human touch.

I did not go to class but was invited by the Armenian to his house. He was a gentle soul and a religious man. His hair was jet black, he had a black moustache, and his skin was pale. He was not handsome but he was spiritual, and his black eyes reflected this. After that we met on a number of occasions, but it was too painful for both of us and we ended our friendship. I used this spiritual fall as a tool to return to God by overcoming the passion that I felt by stricter religious observance.

Chapter 9
Jericho

Jewish prayer was originally informal and spoken from the heart, but then a set order of daily prayers was instituted, and after the destruction of the Temple in Jerusalem, the prayer services became a substitute for the sacrificial offerings that took place twice a day. An additional evening service was added, and consequently Jews pray three times a day according to that set order.

I prayed three times a day but added a prayer from the heart, asking God to change me. But as the years passed, I was disappointed because God was not helping me. I went to a psychiatrist for help but convinced him, and myself, that I was attracted to women. I masturbated to release the tension, but to avoid thoughts of men while masturbating I forced myself to think of women – *as if* these thoughts were better.

And I ended up thinking of men anyway.

I fell to great depths. I considered my thoughts no better than the act itself and the spilling of my seed more severe than all sin. My disappointment turned to anger. I could not comprehend why God would not help me to change; it did not make sense to me.

After all, I was praying for something that God wanted, so why would He not make me a heterosexual?

I cried my heart out when my prayers were not answered. I felt shame that I was still a single man, and I gradually began to break away from the community. I prayed at home alone, and I spent time in nature. Occasionally I drove down to the Dead Sea, taking with me my box of watercolour paints.

On one of my painting trips I took the Roman route that runs parallel to Wadi Kelt, a valley that cuts through the Judaean Desert from Jerusalem to Jericho, and when driving down the meandering road I discovered St. George's Monastery. I stopped the car to take in the splendid view from above the *wadi*. The monastery was built into the side of a cliff, with turquoise painted domes against a background of brown rock; the turquoise colour dominated the scene, but it was the natural brown rock that seemed to complement the coloured domes. I thought to myself how much I would love to live the life of a hermit there, but as breath-taking as the view was, it was not the scene that I wanted to paint. I continued my descent towards Jericho, one of the oldest cities in the world.

On the steep descent, before the road enters into Jericho, I stopped my car and sat on a rock overlooking some shanty dwellings below; they were a cluster of mud huts. There were two dark skinned children dressed in grubby clothes, playing quietly in the dusty soil, and a single hen pecking at the wayside. Further beyond, there were two palm trees, a reservoir, and a daunting mosque, and in the distance lush agricultural lands in striking yellows and greens. In the very far distance was the Moab mountain range tinted in subdued shades of pink and turquoise.

I decided that this was the scene I would paint.

As I was putting the finishing touch to my painting, a Bedouin Arab walked up to look. At first I felt intimidated by his presence, standing beside me in full Arab dress, but then he introduced himself. He was extremely polite and told me that his name was

Ahmad, *Mukhtar* of the clan that lived in the shanty dwellings that I had just painted. To my great surprise he wore a spotlessly clean, white *Gallabiyah* and a white *Ghutra* head scarf. But what was even more surprising, when he shook hands, I noticed that his nails were manicured and he wore a fragrance of musk. His dark skin was as smooth as silk and his green eyes were the colour of new grass.

Ahmad sat down on the rock beside me and gave me an account of his life and the clan that he belonged to. When speaking, he rested his large hand on my knee in a friendly gesture, and I was enchanted by the way he smiled, displaying a perfect set of white teeth. He was very friendly and insisted that I come to his house to drink tea. Although I initially hesitated, I could see no reason why not, and I agreed. He helped me pack up my things, and we walked down the hill to the dwellings below. As we walked past the mud huts, he described to me how they make the bricks from mud and straw, and how they are left out to dry in the sun.

As we entered through an old wooden gate, I felt that we were entering into another world; it was a private enclave, completely fenced-in with mud bricks, and unusually peaceful inside. His house, however, was built with cement building-blocks and consisted of three individual rooms, each with its own entrance. There was a large porch in front, and on the left side an open kitchen. On the right side there stood a separate building which was the *madafa*, a place where guests were received, and it was to this room that he took me. But before we entered the *madafa*, he showed me his garden which he referred to as his *bustan.* He took great pride in his *bustan*, and showed me some very impressive examples of his expertise in the grafting of trees.

Inside the *madafa* there were several colourful mattresses and cushions scattered over a bare concrete floor. We sat cross-legged on a mattress, and I noticed that the walls were raw cement building-blocks, left bare and without plaster. But then Ahmad's wife appeared and stood smiling shyly at the entrance to the *madafa*. She wore a traditional black Bedouin robe and black scarf. When Ahmad introduced me to his wife Miryam, she covered her hand with a scarf before shaking hands which, he told me afterwards, was because she was in a state of purity for praying and was not permitted to touch a man. Ahmad's two little girls entered and dutifully shook hands with me too. They clearly loved their father very much and indeed he was kind and respectful towards them, as he was to his wife.

Miryam made us tea and the two little girls served us and then left. The tea was dark and sweet, flavoured with fresh sage leaves, and served in tiny little glasses. As we chatted about our lives, Ahmad refilled the little glasses again and again, each time welcoming me with the words *ahlan wa-sahlan*. He said that I was invited to stay with him for as long as I like, and he seemed truly happy to have me as his guest.

Ahmad took me to meet his eldest brother Abdullah and his two wives. They lived in a walled-in enclave like Ahmad, but in a mud building with a thatched roof of date palms. It was quite primitive looking, built with mud bricks, and yet it was much more appealing than Ahmad's home built with cement building-blocks. We entered Abdallah's room and I was introduced to him and both his wives. It was customary to drink tea with them, so we sat down while the tea cooked on a fire of twigs at the entrance to the room with the aroma of burning wood floating in. One of Abdullah's wives poured us tea from a burnt, black tea pot and the strong black tea seemed flavoured with smoke — but it was delicious.

Just as the sun was setting we returned to the *madafa*, but Ahmad asked me whether I could eat bread and olives with him. He asked me because of Jewish dietary laws, but I replied that I could, and that I would like to very much. I sat down once again in a cross-legged position, on one of the many colourful mattresses in the *madafa*, while Ahmad served me freshly baked bread with green olives and olive oil. We ate our meal from one dish, dipping the warm and crispy bread into strong flavoured, bitter olive oil, and he told me all about his life as a school teacher, some forty kilometres away in the Judaean Desert where he lived in a tent.

Ahmad invited me to visit him there in his tent, but before I left he insisted on making me Bedouin coffee. He ground the coffee beans with cardamom using a mortar and pestle, and then he cooked it in a brass pot on an open fire inside the *madafa*. The room filled with smoke and we drank the bitter coffee from tiny porcelain cups, sitting close to the glowing cinders of burning wood. I was reminded of the Patriarch Abraham, known for his hospitality in the Book of Genesis, and of his son Ishmael, regarded as ancestor of the Bedouin tribes in the desert. I was convinced that Ahmad must be a descendant of Abraham.

Chapter 10
The same God

Occasionally I drove to Bethlehem to do my shopping. It was like travelling to another country, but in reality it was only a ten minute drive from East Talpiot. I was fascinated when shopping with Arabs in the grocery stores situated along the main road, and on one of my trips I even visited the Church of the Nativity to see the birthplace of Jesus. I also visited Solomon's Pools, close to Bethlehem, which are three large pools with inspiring views of the Judaean Desert.

In Ecclesiastes, known as *Kohelet* in the Hebrew Bible and attributed to King Solomon, it is written:

I made myself pools from which to water the forest of growing trees.

The forest at Solomon's Pools was a mysterious meeting place for young Arab men who, like lovers, could be seen sitting together in parked cars or strolling arm in arm by the pool side.

The pools are fed by local springs and are part of a sophisticated system, of tunnels and aqueducts, built by Herod the Great in connection with the renovations he made to the Second

Temple in Jerusalem, and also which brought water to his palace at Herodium. The aqueduct from Solomon's Pools runs past the apartment building where I lived in East Talpiot, on its way to the Temple Mount in Jerusalem.

One of my favourite walks on the Sabbath was to follow the ruins of the ancient aqueduct from East Talpiot upriver towards Bethlehem. Along the way I stopped to rest under one of the many olive trees that grew down in the valley, and while in the shade of the tree I was able to observe Arab farmers tilling their land with ancient-looking ploughs pulled by donkeys.

It was like being in another world when on the Arab side.

Indeed, I was intrigued by the Arab side and decided to visit Ahmad somewhere in the Judaean Desert. To get to him I drove on the Way of the Patriarchs road, passing Rachel's Tomb in Bethlehem. I stopped my car at the town of Beit Sahour to admire the view of the fertile plateau, so lush and magnificent, and I truly felt that I was in Biblical times. When I looked out over the fields, I imagined Ruth the Moabite gleaning the barley field that belonged to Boaz on that very same land.

I continued on in the direction of Herodium where I had directions how to get to Ahmad, but I realised that I was driving around in circles and had lost my way. It was hot and I was tired, so I stopped my car to take a rest under the shade of an old oak tree. I lay cradled in the roots of the tree and played with the acorns while inhaling a fascinating woody aroma of oak bark, and I was content just lying on the cool ground peering up at the translucent green leaves against the midday sun. Except for the sound of birds and the occasional fly, it was perfectly still and quiet in the heat of the day. I pulled on the blades of grass and chewed on the stalks, enjoying the sweet flavour and completely forgot about Ahmad.

But a gust of wind blew, and then the leaves rustled revealing the blue sky beyond, and a bird fluttered. The breeze brought with it the faint sound of bleating goats, and I stood up to navigate my hearing towards the distant sound. It was far away, but I got my bearings.

I drove along a dirt track and came to a stream where I parked my car and paddled across. The hills were green after the rainy season and as I walked on, the stench of goat's urine told me I was getting closer. I heard voices and could clearly hear the bleating of goats, and suddenly a couple of barking dogs appeared. I had come upon a settlement of Bedouin tents.

As I approached the first tent, a Bedouin woman kneading dough looked up, a tiny child stopped playing in the dirt, and then a man appeared from one of the tents. It was Ahmad, and he recognised me immediately.

"My friend, my friend!" he cried, jumping with joy. He laughed out loud and kissed me on both cheeks, but then he took hold of my hand and led me into the tent. To my astonishment I faced a classroom full of Bedouin school children, and only then did I realise that this was the school that Ahmad had told me about. Each row of desks represented a different year, and Ahmad taught all the subjects, to all the pupils, of all years, together in one classroom – which was a tent! The strikingly beautiful, dark-skinned Bedouin children sat big-eyed, their black hair neatly combed, and they wore clothes of bright colours.

Ahmad introduced me in the English language — for he was also their English teacher.

"This is my friend. His name is Yonatan," he said, proudly.

The children giggled in embarrassment.

Ahmad explained to his pupils in Arabic that I was his guest and that he would bring me to school with him the next morning. He ended class, but first he instructed them to say "good afternoon" to me, and then he took me to his tent.

We found Maryam sweeping the area around their tent, but Ahmad clapped his hands and told her to make tea. His tent contained mattresses, cushions and blankets piled up high. In one corner he kept a Jerrycan where he washed before prayers, and he showed me with great pride how the waste water was channelled outside to irrigate his herb garden.

Ahmad asked me to sit outside while he made his ablutions, and so I took off my sandals and sat cross-legged on the mattress outside, watching Maryam at work. She arranged some leaves and twigs and balanced a charred teapot on three rocks, and then lit the leaves. I watched how she blew gently onto the fire until all the twigs were burning, but at the same time I was listening to Ahmad reciting prayers in his tent. The smoke drifted over with an opulent wood fragrance.

When Ahmad had finished praying he picked mint from his herb garden and stirred a few leaves into the teapot. He poured the tea into little glasses while telling me about his clan and nomadic way of life. I sipped the sweet tincture-like tea with its distinct and strong flavour while listening to his stories, while watching Maryam prepare the bread. She made dough, dusted a wood plank with flour, and put cakes of the dough upon it. She then placed a concave metal disc over a fire and took a cake of dough in her hands, spun it in the air until it took on a thin flat shape, and threw it onto the concave metal disc to bake. Their way of life was a joy to watch.

In the evening Maryam served eggs, goat's cheese and olives, and we ate with our hands. The soft touch of freshly baked bread between my fingertips, the yellow of the yolk, and the dark green of olives set against the white goat's cheese suddenly appeared intense. My senses felt sharpened to the gentle sound of goats, to the calm of smouldering twigs, and the aroma of freshly baked bread dipped in olive oil. Even the mint flavoured tea tasted exceptionally delicious, and in a short time my whole perception of life seemed to change. I observed the simplicity of the scene before my eyes, and it truly gave me a spiritual uplifting.

When it was time for me to sleep, Ahmad covered me with a blanket while I lay under the stars. I felt happy sleeping outside, by the entrance to Ahmad's tent, and yet tears came to my eyes. I recalled my life which in comparison to his was stifling and unnatural. I fell asleep watching the red glow of fire, and I awoke to the sound of Ahmad praying in the middle of the night, and I felt reassured knowing that he was close by.

When morning broke, Ahmad rose for morning prayers and put a jug of water and a towel next to my bed for me to wash. I lay there looking at the heap of grey ashes, where the fire had burned down, and I rose – completely dressed for I had slept in my clothes – and took the jug and towel into a field to answer the call of nature.

When I returned I wrapped myself in my prayer shawl and recited:

How precious is Your kindness, God; the children of men take refuge in the shadow of Your wings.
They will be filled from the abundance of Your house, and from the stream of Your delights You will give them to drink.
For with You is the source of life, in Your light we see light.
Extend Your kindness to those who know You, and Your righteousness to the upright in heart.

I then put on my *Tefillin* and prayed, with Ahmad praying to the same God.

We had breakfast, and sweet tea, and afterwards we walked to Ahmad's school. He opened the tent and prepared himself for class and, as the children began to arrive, he greeted each one of them with a beaming smile like a proud father. I noticed that they also responded with beaming smiles, and I chuckled because in fact they all belonged to one big extended family – the *hamula*.

Ahmad asked each pupil to say his name in English:

"My name is Muhammad!"

"My name is Hussein!"

"My name is Amina!"

And so it went on until the last student.

"*Mumtaz!*" exclaimed Ahmad, beaming with joy.

I told Ahmad that I wanted to take a walk in nature, but in truth I was getting emotional watching them and their happiness. I walked for hours, recalling my unhappy childhood, and my unhappy schooling. When I finally returned to Ahmad's school, he had already finished class for the day.

As we walked to his tent, he announced that he was taking me on a trip, and that we were going on his two donkeys. I roared with laughter at the thought of this, but he explained that the purpose of the trip was to find *hubeza* – mallow – a plant that grows after the rainy season, and which we needed for our evening meal.

Along the way we found various herbs, of which Ahmad knew each one by its name and medicinal properties. We rode upon the donkeys at a slow pace, through streams and past caves, and stopped where the *hubeza* grew. We cut as much as was needed and continued riding on, stopping for herbs along the way, and then we found a quiet spot to rest. Ahmad tied up the donkeys, took out a kettle to make tea, and gathered some twigs. We sat around a fire with the birds chirping and the bees buzzing, drinking sweet tea in the middle of nature.

Later that evening we ate a meal of *hubeza* with bread. Afterwards I tasted all the different herbal drinks which Ahmad had prepared, with him instructing me on each of their medicinal properties. The evening was quiet, and the fire burned down to a grey cinder, but then Ahmad took out a *rebab*, a home-made musical instrument, which was square in shape and covered in parchment with three strings.

Ahmad played the *rebab* with a bow, but then he began singing in hypnotic harmony to the sounds of the *rebab*. I was mesmerized by the sounds and lay down on the mattress, gazing up at the countless stars, while listening to traditional Bedouin songs sung in Ahmad's guttural voice, in the same way as was once sung by ancient desert dwellers.

The stars appeared exceptionally bright and beautiful in the dark of the night. I do not know whether it was due to Ahmad's singing voice, or whether it was the herbal drinks that I had drunk, that made everything seem so lovely. I drifted off into a trance and the next thing I recall was absolute silence — and I felt Ahmad covering me with a blanket. I slept soundly until the morning.

And so the days passed.

The time came, however, for me to return to Jerusalem and prepare for the Sabbath. Ahmad invited me to visit him again, at his home in Jericho. Before I left, he asked me politely to come and say goodbye to the pupils at his school-in-a-tent.

Chapter 11
Beersheba

I received a job offer with the Swiss airline in Beersheba, but it meant that I would have to travel through Judea and Samaria, the West Bank, to get to work each day. I was familiar with the area from my army service and knew that I would have to travel through Hebron and Halhul; the intifada uprising was in full force, and already on the journey to my interview my car was pelted with rocks. I therefore decided to rent an additional apartment in Beersheba.

Beersheba is the capital of the Negev Desert and since Biblical times, when Abraham and Isaac dug wells there, it has remained the land of the nomad. The Bedouins live a nomadic lifestyle and I was enchanted to see them gathered at the weekly Bedouin market in Beersheba, selling their sheep and camels in a way I imagined was done in Biblical times.

The airline office was located in the old city of Beersheba in the picturesque Turkish Quarter, in an old house built in the Ottoman period. The neighbourhood was delightful, but the office was quiet with nothing much for me to do except twiddle my thumbs all day long. After a few weeks in Beersheba I began to feel bored and regretted having made the move.

Then, one evening, when I filled up my car with petrol at the local petrol station, the Bedouin petrol attendant asked me if I was an artist.

"In actual fact I do paint watercolours," I answered. "How did you know?"

"I can tell because I am also an artist and I felt that you are too," he said.

I was somewhat dubious and could not help ask, in a tone of irony: "*You're* an artist?"

The Bedouin boy laughed, showing a set of stained and uneven teeth. He informed me that he had attended a Jewish school in Beersheba, had won prizes for his art work, and had travelled to the United States to represent his school. He spoke of the High Renaissance, of artists Raphael, Michelangelo and Leonardo Da Vinci, and expressed his love for the Mona Lisa. He told me that he had to work as a petrol attendant to earn a living, but at home he has his own studio. The young Bedouin invited me to his home to see his work and to meet his family.

When I arrived to the illegal township where Ishmael lived, I was troubled by what I saw. The people lived in tents, but because they were prevented from living the life of a nomad they built dwellings out of scrap materials – such as rusty tin sheets, asbestos, old doors, metal sign posts, plastic, and even pieces of carton. The illegal township was overcrowded, there were no roads, no collection of garbage, and there was a stench of open sewage. I saw rats as large as cats roaming around freely and it appeared that the citizens did not care. They lived in squalor.

Nomadic tribes ruled the Negev desert for hundreds of years prior to the State of Israel. They moved through the desert in search of grazing land but after the establishment of the State of Israel a new law limited their movement, and subsequently they were forced to give up their livelihood as shepherds and settled down in illegal townships, of which Ishmael's was one of the many, without electricity, without running water, and without municipality services.

I found Ishmael waiting for me outside a hovel. It was heartbreaking for me to see this young man greet me in such appalling conditions. He was of slim build and wore blue jeans with a white T-shirt that hung from his broad shoulders. His face was sunburnt from the hot desert sun and his curly jet-black hair was askew. He welcomed me with a kiss on both cheeks, and with a big smile on his face he took me to meet his family.

We went along a path of broken tiles, alongside open drainage, to an outside kitchen where his mother was cooking on a dirty gas ring, connected to a gas canister by a long rubber pipe. She was an elderly lady dressed in a traditional black Bedouin dress with red embroidery. Ishmael introduced me and then took me to meet his brothers who were laying on mattresses and smoking *nargileh* water pipes around a smouldering fire, in an outside living room. All the brothers stood up to shake hands with me and then made a place for me to lie down snugly between them. They deliberately left no room for Ishmael, and teased him that they had kidnapped me.

Never before had I encountered such provocative looking men; each one with a splendid physique and wearing tight fitting jeans. There was something erotic about them, with their voluptuous bodies sprawled over each other, each one using the other as a pillow. In no time I found myself sandwiched between them, and I became a pillow too. I began to wonder if I was in a male harem. We drank tea in this uncomfortable reclining position, but they finally freed me so that I could go to see Ishmael's artwork.

Ishmael's studio was a room made from broken plywood, corrugated iron and old window frames, but large enough to accommodate an industrial work table. When I entered, I noticed that there was a strong smell of oil paint that dominated the room. On the table there were containers of different paint mediums:

tubes of water-colour paint, bottles of acrylic paint, and tins of oil paint. There were various paint brushes, knives, and pots, but amongst all the mess there was an impressive bust sculpture that Ishmael had made.

The plywood floor creaked loudly as we moved around and I was curious to know why he had two refrigerators in the room; after all, there was no electricity. Ishmael opened up both refrigerators to reveal piles of books and paintings inside, which was the only way he could keep everything hermetically sealed to prevent the rats from eating them.

Ishmael was a gifted young man and indeed a true artist. He suggested that we meet again to find a spot somewhere so that we could sketch together. This we did on a number of occasions, and afterwards we would compare our work and then go back to the brothers' harem for a pot of tea.

After the hot summer, when the winter season came and when the temperatures in the northern part of the Negev Desert dropped, there would be heavy rains causing the dry river beds to flood. From time to time I visited Ishmael and his brothers on those dark winter nights, drawn to them by their warm hospitality — and their affectionate behaviour.

On one occasion I drove with my headlights on high-beam illuminating the pelting rain, as if driving through trillions of silver sequins, with the monotonous whining of windscreen wipers going back-and-forth. Inside the car sound was muffled, but outside there was a storm blowing with a distant and eerie sound of corrugated metal flapping in the wind. I saw car inner tubes and corroded bed frames flying off the make-shift roofs, and what had once been a dusty path was now a mud bath.

I found Ishmael's brothers inside a makeshift living room, huddled around a burning fire with gale force winds whistling through the cracks and openings; there were buckets all around the room to catch the rainwater. Ishmael went to do some chores but left me nestled comfortably between his brothers with the rain hammering against the tin roof. I became absorbed in the deep red glow that came from the log fire and the constant bubbling sound from *nargileh* water pipes. All the brothers' eyes were blood-shot from the hot, smoke-filled room. There was a strong aroma of perfumed tobacco, and of stale coffee that came from a brass coffee pot that lay in a heap of grey ashes. The smouldering logs played a meditative crackle but then the magical atmosphere was suddenly disturbed when Ishmael entered the room with tea, and to inform me that my car was bogged down in the mud.

I was stranded with the Bedouins.

"Tonight you are sleeping with me," he said grinning, as his brothers stared enviously with red eyes.

Ishmael's studio, where we went to sleep, was cold and miserable. He threw down two cotton mattresses and went to bed fully clothed, each covered with one thin blanket. My teeth, however, did not stop chattering from the cold so we cuddled up under the two blankets and fell asleep together.

In the middle of the night I was awoken by something biting my ear.

"*Ishmael!*" I shouted.

"What happened, Yonatan?"

"A rat was nibbling my ear!" I cried in horror.

"Yonatan, don't wake me up because of a rat! Wake me *only* if it's a snake," he said, unconcerned. He simply pulled me under the blankets, and we continued sleeping.

Early in the morning one of his brothers came to wake me, and to inform me that the rain had stopped. I got up to have a glass of tea with him and told him about the rat that bit me, and what Ishmael said.

"Maybe it was Ishmael's snake that bit you?" he mumbled.

While in Beersheba, in the enticing company of these friendly men, there were no religious boundaries to keep me from temptation. I tried to live a religious way of life to overcome the temptation. For that reason exactly I allowed myself to be indoctrinated by the strict adherence to *halakha* – Jewish Law. I was forbidden to yield to the desire. I had produced a robot, an Artificial Jew, programmed to perform the 613 commandments — but I was hanging by a thread.

I resigned from my job in Beersheba and returned to a strict, religious way of life in Jerusalem.

Chapter 12
Attacked because I was a Jew

I took a position with the Greek airline in Jerusalem and found fulfilment in my work, and it became the most important thing in my life; I put in long hours and gave my whole self to my work, slipping into a mechanical routine of work and religious observance. But on the weekends I continued going over to the Arab side.

I decided one Friday morning to visit Ahmad at his home in Jericho, and drove through East Jerusalem, via the Old City where there was heavy traffic prior to Friday Prayers at the Al-Aqsa Mosque. I sat in my car, moving at a slow speed with the traffic, while watching the multitude of worshippers streaming towards Damascus Gate. The pavements were lined with vendors and many of the worshippers made last minute purchases on the way to the mosque. I became engrossed in their world as I observed with fascination another culture from the quiet of my car.

The traffic congestion eased and I continued my journey down towards Jericho. Eventually I turned off the highway and drove down the Roman route that runs parallel to Wadi Kelt.

I found Ahmad irrigating his *bustan* and was greeted in his usual cheerful way, with kisses and hugs, and at once he demanded Maryam to make tea — *quickly!* His cheerful manner made me chuckle, and I watched in awe as Maryam ran to make the tea.

Ahmad was very proud of his new home and especially of how his shrubs and trees were progressing in the *bustan*. He even took me to see his new pit-toilet which was a squat toilet, with a large hole in the ground where the excrement and waste decomposed. He showed me the new wash room which he had built especially for his guests, where they could make their ablutions before prayers. The water was siphoned from the aqueduct which ran above. Quite close to the *bustan* were also the ruins of an ancient aqueduct, built by Herod the Great, which had once brought the water supply from Jerusalem through the Judaean Desert to the king's winter palace in Jericho.

After we had our tea we went for a walk to the Aqabat-Jaber refugee camp. Along the way I was introduced to other members of the clan who lived in the refugee camp in houses of mud bricks. But Ahmad had a younger brother named Khalil who did not live in a house of mud bricks, but lived in a charming cottage surrounded by a garden filled with flowers and herbs.

Khalil was a pedantic young man who constantly applied cream to his hands, his hair was neatly parted on one side, and he had a small clipped moustache. He had similar features as Ahmad, the same smooth dark skin and the same green eyes, but he wore western clothes with a jacket and a tie, all perfectly pressed. His cottage was furnished in western styled furnishings, and he awaited just a bride.

Ahmad then took me to see the school where he taught, in a large white building run by UNRWA (United Nations Relief and Works Agency) especially for the Palestinian refugees, although most of the people in the refugee camp, including Ahmad's clan, were not refugees at all.

We strolled back to Ahmad's *bustan*, meeting other members of the clan along the way, and it suddenly occurred to me that they all intermarried within the same *hamula*, and that Ahmad's wife was actually his cousin. The clan was spread out over different parts of Jericho, and in fact as far as Hebron. I learnt, however, that a few families from his *hamula* lived in Wadi Kelt, alongside the aqueduct that brings the water to Jericho, and decided that on my next trip into nature I would visit them there.

As it was getting late, and I still had to prepare for the Sabbath, I drove home by the same route that I had come by. Once again there was heavy traffic at Damascus Gate except that this time the worshippers were going home, after Friday Prayers. The traffic came to a complete standstill and I realized that I was a sitting duck, stuck in a traffic jam. The worshippers saw me with my yarmulke on my head, and with a look of hatred in their eyes pelted my car with rocks. A rock came crashing through the windscreen window and hit me in the face; I was wearing glasses and froze with fear, but when I felt the blood trickling down my face there was only one thing for me to do.

I ran for my life.

I left my car in the middle of the traffic and ran through the crowds towards the mounted police. They saw the blood, but they instructed me to go back to my car and steered their horses behind me. I had to wade through crowds of people, but I was protected by the mounted police behind me. I finally got into my car and was led to safety by them. I needed medical attention but my only concern was not to be late for the Sabbath, so I drove home as I was.

On the journey home everyone was staring at my smashed up car and my bloodied face. I did not have time to prepare any food for Shabbat but ate that evening with a friend in the building. Later that night, when I was alone in the quiet of my apartment, I broke down crying; I did not cry because of the cuts and my black-eye but cried because I had been attacked by Arabs who did not know me — and did not know my soul.

Chapter 13
Wadi Kelt

Religious life had been a joy all the time that there was hope; I honestly believed that God was going to change me, but I suddenly understood that I had been fooling myself all along. I began to hold a grudge against God because things had not turned out the way I expected. In my prayers I broke down crying, and asked: "Why have You abandoned me?" I cried out with unholy thoughts: "I don't believe that there is a God!" and I pulled off my *Tefillin* in anger, proclaiming: "It's a waste of time!"

I felt let down by God.

I was ashamed to be single, and even though I did not have homosexual relationships I knew that I had not changed. I was not heterosexual and did not feel any attraction towards women. I loathed myself because of it and begged God to help me change, but God rejected me. I therefore speculated that I must be worthless in His eyes, and if I was worthless I may as well have been dead.

And yet the Jewish way of life remained very much a part of me. I was still an observant Jew, and like many other observant Jews I went through the motions from the moment I got up in the morning till the time that I went to bed at night. Indeed, I lived a life according to *halakha* – Jewish law. I put on *Tefillin*, I prayed three times a day, I blessed my food before eating, and I said Grace after my meals. Twice a day I recited the *Shema*:

Hear, O Israel, the Lord is our God, the Lord is One.
Blessed be the name of his glorious Majesty forever and ever.
Love the Lord your God with all your heart, with all your soul, with all your means.
And these words which I command you today shall be upon your heart.
Teach them diligently to your children.
And talk of them when you sit in your house, when you walk on the road, when you lie down and when you rise up.
Bind them for a sign upon your hand and for frontlets between your eyes.
Write them upon the doorposts of your house and upon your gates.

When I recited the words, however, I broke down crying. The words were supposed to remind me of my obligation to God, and cautioned me against going astray. What is more, I could not teach them diligently to my children because I did not have children to teach: I was cursed! Indeed, I would never have a family of my own.

I was deeply hurt. And yet, I continued living a Jewish way of life and lived for God's Sabbath each week. I aimed for the moment when everything would stop, when the sun set, and when the Sabbath candles were burning. It was the highlight of the week; the moment when there was quiet with just the meditative sound of hot water simmering in the urn. The dining table would be set in my best tableware, with two fresh loaves of white Challah bread ready to be broken over the clean and white tablecloth, and a silver goblet filled with red wine to sanctify the holy day. On Friday nights the apartment was filled with tempting aromas that came from the hot-plate, the stone floors were washed clean, and the sheets on my bed were laundered and scented. *This* was the mechanical way of life that was ingrained in me, and I could live no other way.

However, between work and religious observance, I continued escaping into nature. On one of my trips I decided to seek out Ahmad's clan in Wadi Kelt.

Already, upon my arrival at the top of the *wadi*, my breath was taken away. I looked out over the vast wilderness and saw a dramatic landscape of sun-lit hills with contrasting shadows that multiplied into the distance and faded into the horizon. As I descended into the wadi and immersed myself into the hills, I detected narrow trails hewn by herds of goats that had wandered the hills for decades in search of grazing areas. Embossed against the pale desert hillside, a herd of goats made a zigzag pattern of diagonal trails in rich pigments of browns and black, like a painting on an Egyptian papyrus scroll. The black robe of a Bedouin woman punctuated the desert hills. Finally I came across a green oasis which was home to the Bedouins at the bottom of the *wadi*.

On one side of the *wadi* was Ahmad's father, Muhammad Abu Abdullah, who lived with his second wife and children in a romantic looking building in the middle of the oasis. His first wife, who was Ahmad's mother, lived in Jericho. The building was originally a flourmill built by the prominent Husseini clan of Jerusalem more than a century ago, and sits majestically on the side of the *wadi* where the aqueduct runs from Jerusalem to Jericho. Muhammad Abu Abdullah and his family lived in the upper apartments, level with the aqueduct, in rooms with impressive arched windows and vaulted ceilings. In the lower apartments, on the ground floor, the goats and sheep were housed.

Muhammad Abu Abdullah had been a shepherd all of his life, but was getting on in years. He spent his retirement sitting outside on the roof of the flourmill smoking a *nargileh* and giving orders to his wife and children. When he got angry he jumped up and used his walking stick to beat them. His skin, scorched black from the blazing hot sun, sagged loosely over his bones and was kept supple with olive oil.

Muhammad Abu Abdullah's second wife was a friendly old woman named Helwa who looked tired and haggard. When I visited them, she welcomed the chance to take a break from her chores and to make tea. While the tea was cooking on the fire she rolled a cigarette, twisting the end tightly to seal it, and then lit her creation. The end flared up as she sucked hard on it, drawing the smoke down into her lungs, and she appeared deep in thought: she gazed into the distance, holding the hand-rolled cigarette between her long, dark and wrinkled fingers – the nails were black with dirt – and began telling me stories about her life in the *wadi*. I was surprised to see that she had only two teeth.

After I drank my tea I crossed over to the other side of the *wadi* to visit Ahmad's sister, Fatimah. She lived with her husband Suleiman, together with his second wife and all his children from both wives, in an abandoned pumping station. It was a nondescript building built in the time of the British Mandate. Fatimah was dressed in a traditional Islamic tunic with a white hijab, tied tightly around her head. She avoided physical contact but was friendly and hospitable, constantly praising God – *Alhamdulillah* – and swept away the dirt to put down a mattress for me to sit upon. She went to prepare a pot of tea, and I sat on the mattress thinking to myself how different their tempo of life was to mine; the Bedouins were calm and patient and the measurement of time did not seem to have any meaning to them. I waited, somewhat impatiently, for yet another pot of tea in the *wadi*, while watching the children play.

The children were a scruffy bunch, all of them with runny noses and flies clinging to the mucous. They played barefoot in the dirt, and the boys ran around completely naked. I was astonished when one little boy squat down in the dirt and defecated right in front of me but then continued playing as if nothing had happened.

Fatimah saw that I had my camera with me and asked if I would take some photographs. Naturally I was happy to oblige, so she ran off with all the children to change their clothes. I drank my tea while admiring the flourmill's architecture on the other side of the *wadi*. Suddenly Fatimah appeared in a glittering silver gown with a floral patterned head scarf, and the children were dressed in clean clothes and sandals, with their hair wetted and combed.

They all posed for a photograph in the dirt.

I continued on, following the aqueduct down towards St. George's Monastery. It was a delight to see the monastery from down in the *wadi*; I had previously admired it from the Roman route above, when I visited Ahmad in Jericho. I was now able to observe from close-up the Greek Orthodox monks in black cassocks and *kalimavkion* head coverings against the cluster of white buildings with turquoise-coloured domes and verandas and red rooftops built into the side of the gorge.

What could be better than to live the life of a hermit in a room above the canyon, having no contact with the outside world, and to be completely alone with God? I could very easily have lived their ancient way of life in the desert, and I wished that I could find peace in the way that they did. I seriously wondered to myself whether I should have become a monk and envisioned myself serving God in a tranquil existence in the desert.

As I walked back along the aqueduct, I was deep in thought. I wondered what kept me from happiness and began to envy the monks' religious way of life in the desert. But I chuckled when I realised that I *had* found happiness right there and then: nature is God's creation, and I found God when in nature but not in a synagogue!

When I arrived back at the old pumping station I was introduced to Fatima's husband Suleiman. He was a friendly fellow, albeit somewhat disagreeable in appearance. He was shaving outside, using a dirty, chipped cup filled with boiling water and dipped the razor with his right hand while holding a jagged, broken mirror in the other. He was a skinny man with a pinched, tired face. His small, beady brown eyes were set in dark sockets, he had grey hair but was balding, and his teeth were long and black. In some uncanny way, when he laughed, he reminded me of a donkey.

Suleiman worked for the Israel Nature and Parks Authority, and it was his job to scout the whole of the *wadi*. He therefore knew the area very well and suggested that we go to bathe in a pool nearby. I was under the impression that because he was a Bedouin he would be a lover of nature, but he was not. When I stopped to admire the wild flowers, or simply to share with him the way the water flowed over the rocks, he did not see the beauty that I saw.

We finally came to a pool and waded through the water, between the deep and narrow gorge, but he took me even further up the *wadi* to yet another pool with a magnificent waterfall. The water was ice cold but we both went for a swim. Suleiman then made his ablutions and we returned to the old pumping station.

I was enchanted by Wadi Kelt and when Suleiman invited me to come to stay with him and his family, I told him that I would like that very much and promised to return.

Chapter 14
The Hebrew Calendar

The Intifada ended, and the Oslo Accords were officially signed at a Washington ceremony hosted by President Bill Clinton. Yitzhak Rabin shook hands with Yasser Arafat and there was hope of peace. But then there was a series of fatal terrorist attacks including two Jewish boys who were murdered in Wadi Kelt.

During the following year the Palestinian Authority was formed and Yasser Arafat, Shimon Peres and Yitzhak Rabin were jointly awarded the Nobel Peace Prize. And finally that year, Israel and Jordan signed a Treaty of Peace for normalization between the two countries — but there were more fatal terrorist attacks and the beginning of Palestinian suicide bombings.

I thrived in my new job with the Greek airline and was praised by the General Manager in Tel Aviv. However, the peace process created changes: in the Jerusalem office, where I worked, my Palestinian colleague was made manager and another Palestinian joined the staff. The atmosphere in the office changed dramatically and then, much to my astonishment, the General Manager in Tel Aviv informed me that he had received complaints about me from the Palestinian sector. Evidently the Palestinians did not want me there.

The terrorist attacks and suicide bombings continued, and the following year two more Jewish boys were murdered while hiking in Wadi Kelt.

The Greek airline had a company dinner on November 4, 1995 — 12th of *Heshvan* on the Hebrew Calendar — but as we were nearing the end of the meal, reports began to come in that Yitzhak Rabin had been assassinated. There was shock and confusion, and even embarrassment with the Palestinian staff; the general opinion was that it was another Palestinian terrorist attack. I suggested, however, that it was the Jews who did it and the Jewish staff looked at me in disgust.

The autumn season ended and Jerusalem grew cold. Clouds filled the sky, casting a shadow over the Old City walls, and what was once the golden shimmer of the Dome of the Rock shrine was now a dark silhouette against a grey sky.

The rains came and washed the dust and grime away, lending the Old City a subdued and more serious character; and as I looked out over the dramatic landscape of grey neutrals, of wet reflections and blackness, I was reminded of the English landscape artist Bonington.

Then winter came and it was bitterly cold. Walking through the deep snow I discovered that the trees lining the streets had broken from the weight of snow. The wet trunks and branches lay black and motionless in the snow, like dying souls laid out in white burial shrouds. From a deserted hill I looked out over a white Jerusalem lost in snow; a nonentity where nothing stirred except the raven's black plumage against a cold infinity.

Towards the end of the Hebrew month of *Kislev*, when the days are at their shortest, the eight-day holiday of *Hanukah* commenced. *Hanukah* is a holiday that commemorates the re-dedication of the Temple to the service of God after it had been defiled with paganism. It is a festival of light and hope to all those in despair.

On the tenth day of the month of *Tevet*, a fast commemorates the beginning of the siege of Jerusalem by the armies of Nebuchadnezzar, King of Babylon, and prayers of repentance are recited.

In the following month of *Shvat* the hills in and around Jerusalem became splashes of pink from the blossoming of almond trees: it was the New Year for trees. I recall the time when I used to sit on the hill in the shade of a tree, painting a view of the Old City to the tranquil sound of tin bells that came from the flocks of sheep. A shepherd paused to inquire about my painting and complimented me on my work, but an elaborate promenade has been built upon that hill and instead of sheep, flocks of people now wander by.

I could not find peace anymore on the hill that I had once loved so much, so I wandered down to the Jerusalem Peace Forest where the ground was carpeted in pine-needles. The woody pine fragrance rose up, and cyclamens showed their inquisitive little faces. I lay on the ground looking up, through the tall pine-trees into a blue sky; and there I found peace, with God's rays of light penetrating through.

In the month of *Adar* there is a fast day before the celebration of *Purim*. *Purim* commemorates the miraculous deliverance of the Jewish people from Ahasuerus, King of Persia, and the entertaining story is read from the Scroll of Esther. On this day it is customary to hold a banquet with alcoholic beverages.

In the month of *Nisan*, *Pesach* – the festival of Passover – is celebrated in commemoration of the deliverance of the Children of Israel from Egyptian bondage. God promised "to pass over you, and there shall no plague be upon you". On that day the Passover Lamb was to be roasted and eaten in haste with unleavened bread. In the Torah, the Festival of the Unleavened Bread is to be kept as a memorial on the fifteenth day in the month of *Abib*, which means the month of spring, but was later named the month of *Nisan*. The festival tells the story of the exodus, which happened over 3000 years ago, and is read from the *Haggadah*, a textbook that contains the order of the service — the *Seder* — together with a ritual meal.

The festival of Passover is the time to spring-clean and "put away leaven out of your houses". Having removed all the leaven from the house, one then changes all the pots and pans, dishes and cutlery, and eats only food that is Kosher for Passover.

Passover was also the start of the barley harvest when a special peace offering was made, and forty-nine days were counted, connecting Passover to the wheat offering on the festival of *Shavuot* — the Feast of Weeks — the fiftieth day. This period is known as the *Counting of the Omer*. (*Omer* is a unit of measure for grain.)

In the month of *Sivan*, *Shavuot* – the Feast of Weeks – is observed after the *Counting of the Omer* period. In the Torah it is referred to as the Festival of Harvest, for it marks the harvesting of the wheat and the Day of the First Fruits when the Israelites brought a thanksgiving offering to God. However, in the prayer book, the festival is referred to as the Season of the Giving of our Torah, but it is chiefly associated with the *receiving* of the Torah at Mount Sinai, namely the Ten Commandments — the heart of the 613 Commandments.

In the meantime, in the month of *Iyar*, Israel's Independence Day is celebrated. Although it is a secular holiday, some synagogues have special prayers of thanksgiving to God. In the same month of *Iyar*, Jerusalem Day is celebrated to commemorate the reunification of Jerusalem and the return of Jewish sovereignty for the first time since the destruction of the Second Temple in the year 70.

Finally summer arrived, and on the seventeenth day of the month of *Tamuz* a fast day marks the first breach in the city walls during the Babylonian siege. There is then a three week mourning period up until the ninth day of the month of *Av*, which is also a fast day. The Ninth of *Av* fast day is the saddest and most tragic day of the year. It commemorates the destruction of both the First Temple, by the Babylonians, and the Second Temple in 70 C.E. by the Romans.

The fast days, with the many restrictions involved in laws of mourning, were a burden for me. And if that was not enough, the Hebrew month of *Elul* was approaching, which was the last month of the year, and a month in preparation for the Days of Awe — a period of repentance and prayer.

It seemed that I was forever fasting and mourning, repenting and praying, and yet none of this helped me.

On the first day of the Hebrew month of *Tishre*, *Rosh Hashanah* – the Jewish New Year – is celebrated. In the Torah *Tishre* is the seventh month of the year, and there is no reference to *Rosh Hashanah*. In the Torah, the first day of *Tishre* is referred to as the Day of Remembrance, or Day of Sounding the Horn, a memorial day proclaimed with the blast of horns. No work is done on this day and it is a solemn day saddened by the confession of one's sins. Nonetheless, the day is a festival – and it is observed for two days — and the day after is yet another fast day.

Rosh Hashanah marks the beginning of the Ten Days of Penitence that prepares us for the fast of *Yom Kippur* – the Day of Atonement – the holiest day in the year.

There was not enough time for hikes in nature because I had to spend my time in prayer asking for forgiveness. My High Holyday prayer book for *Rosh Hashanah* and *Yom Kippur* had more than five hundred pages of prayers; my Sabbath prayer book had three hundred pages and my daily prayer book had two hundred pages. Prayer was a routine of recitations said with the congregation in a rushed fashion and I found no spiritual uplifting whatsoever.

But then, four days after *Yom Kippur,* came the festival of *Sukkot* – the Feast of Tabernacles.

Sukkot is a festival of joy when the Jewish people move into a temporary hut for seven days to reenact the way the Children of

Israel had lived in the desert during their years of wandering after the exodus from Egypt. It is also a reminder of God's protection in the desert, when God provided manna and water, and that we in turn must be grateful for all we have.

The festival of *Sukkot* is agricultural in origin and referred to as the Festival of the Ingathering, in the Torah. What is especially motivating about this festival, however, is the commandment to take a citron, a palm branch, a myrtle branch and a willow branch – and to rejoice!

In preparation for the festival I went to Mea Shearim to purchase the Four Plants.

Mea Shearim is a neighbourhood in Jerusalem that takes one back in time to the Eastern European Shtetl; a pious community that adhered to Jewish Law. Likewise, in Mea Shearim, traditional dress is prominent and large posters forbid women from entering the community wearing immodest clothing.

Before the festival of *Sukkot*, the streets in Mea Shearim are lined with vendors selling the Four Plants – the citron, the palm branch, the myrtle branch and the willow branch. Also for sale are ready-made temporary huts to dwell in, and decorations to decorate the temporary huts.

I found the atmosphere of buying and selling to be exciting and indeed joyous, especially after the solemn period that we had just passed. As I strolled around observing the ultra-Orthodox Jews dressed in their black suits and wide-brimmed hats — some of them in long black frock-coats of satin, some in three-quarter length jackets, knee-breeches and white socks — I noticed that they were inspecting the citrons with magnifying glasses and measuring the branches with rulers. I watched in disbelief, and I felt angered; they were taking the beauty out of nature by bringing it down to a technicality. I decided then and there to purchase the Four Plants and leave, but when I heard the exorbitant prices, I said to myself, "It's a swindle!" and left in a huff.

Chapter 15
The First day of Sukkot

I was invited by my friend Joel to spend the first day of the *Sukkot* festival with him. At first I hesitated because I had felt resentment after the protest rallies that he participated in and because of the general atmosphere of hatred it caused at the time. We argued after the assassination, but Joel maintained that he didn't want Yitzhak Rabin murdered. "I just wanted him to die," he said.

He and his wife were good people; modern Orthodox Jews who were strictly observant. Joel wore a knitted yarmulke, did not have a beard, and dressed in regular clothing. His wife wore a beret and dressed modestly and with decency, according to Jewish law. Joel, in particular, was open-minded and, although younger than me by fifteen years, I looked up to him. I wanted to be married like him, and I wanted a home based on Torah like his. He already had five children at the time, and I was impressed by the way that they raised their children, discussing with them Biblical stories at the Sabbath table.

I met Joel and Nomi while I was on a trip to the United States, when they were engaged to be married. After they married they came to live in Israel, in East Talpiot, but they then moved to Maaleh Adumim, a new Israeli city in Judea and Samaria built atop the red mountainous heights that ascend from the Dead Sea. Up until the time of Yitzhak Rabin's assassination, I often stayed with them for the Sabbath and festivals and always went out to find a quiet spot to meditate — with the spectacular views over the desert landscape.

The first day of the festival of *Sukkot* on this particular year fell on the Sabbath which meant that, according to Jewish law, we were not permitted to touch the Four Plants – the citron, the palm, the myrtle and the willow. Nevertheless, it was a commandment to dwell in the *Sukkah* – the temporary hut – for seven days, including on the Sabbath.

I arrived early so that I could help with the final preparations in the building of the *Sukkah*, but due to the numerous laws involved in the building of a *Sukkah*, such as what constitutes a wall, what is the permissible height, what the roof may be made of, and whether there can be a space between the walls and the roof, I began to wonder how all these rules could possibly be a reminder of God's protection in the desert.

That evening, when I was in synagogue with Joel, I said a private prayer asking God to make me happy. After all, it was the season of rejoicing and I needed to get into a festive mood, but I was feeling one of gloom.

Upon our return from synagogue, the family gathered in the *Sukkah* and recited the necessary prayers and benedictions. There is also a tradition of hospitality, for it is said that it is necessary for man to rejoice in the *Sukkah* and to be cheerful towards his guests. I wondered, however, what my hosts really felt in their inner souls; they were controlled by laws and tradition, and I wondered whether this was really their true personality.

There is yet another tradition on each day of the festival, known as *Ushpizin*, to invite the soul of one of the seven shepherds of Israel: Abraham, Isaac, Jacob, Moses, Aaron, Joseph, and King David. Our guest of honour on the first night was Abraham.

The children were happy, and the *Sukkah* was decorated with plastic fruits and colourful paper chains. As we ate the festive meal, Joel and Nomi asked the children questions relating to the laws of the festival of *Sukkot*, and indeed it was a joyous time. However, I did not feel joy in my heart. As I sat with them in the *Sukkah*, I made a plan.

Then, after Nomi had cleared the table and I had washed the dishes, and the children were already in bed, I announced that I was going to visit some friends.

"I didn't know that you have friends in Maaleh Adumim!" Joel responded with delight.

"I don't! I'm going to walk down to Wadi Kelt," I answered, and watched both their mouths drop.

"That is ridiculous! It's dangerous, it's too far, and I'm going to bed!" said Nomi, and she stormed off.

It was painful knowing that I had upset Nomi but Joel, on the other hand, sat down with me to hear my plan. I told him that I would walk down the red mountainous heights and then go deep down into the ravine to where the Bedouins live. He did not object, and in fact I believe that he secretly liked the idea. I asked him if he would come to collect me the following night, after the Sabbath which was the first day of *Sukkot*, and he was more than happy to oblige.

The first day of *Sukkot* is celebrated on the fifteenth day of the Hebrew month of *Tishre,* which meant that I had the light of a full moon. I descended the mountainside towards the dry and dusty desert, climbing over rocks, through dry weeds and thistles, and past Bedouin encampments where dogs barked at me viciously. Eventually I arrived to the highway and was able to get my bearings; I ran across the road, jumped over the divide, and continued overland until I came to the edge of the deep ravine, which was Wadi Kelt.

Here I stopped to rest, but my head was filled with thoughts and fears. What if the Bedouins would not welcome me? What if I would fall down the ravine? What if I was attacked along the way?

I started my descent down into the ravine but was overcome with melancholy and cried. I saw myself as a lost soul wandering the desert in the middle of the night; a lonely person who did not belong anywhere. All the way down I pleaded with God to help me: I begged Him that Suleiman would be happy to see me — because I feared he would not.

When I reached the bottom of the *wadi*, after hours of walking, the fear of rejection choked me. I stood trancelike, unable to move, as I gazed in dismay at the family of Bedouins sleeping on the rooftop of the old pumping station. The cold moonlight shone upon them as they slept peacefully in their beds, but I felt that it was an invasion of their privacy and I remained standing, completely paralyzed.

Suddenly the dogs barked and everyone woke up. Little haloed heads looked up at me from under the silver moonlight, but then Suleiman jumped up, scratching his head in confusion. The moonlight shone from behind him, illuminating the pure white of his cotton *Gallabiyah*, and my eyes were drawn to the black silhouette of his naked body.

"I'll arrange a place for you to sleep and we'll talk in the morning," he said, shrugging his shoulders. He called to Jasser, his eldest son, and told him to bring me a mattress, and then he went back to sleep.

Jasser brought me a mattress, with a blanket and a pillow, and placed them next to his mattress. He then went to fill me jug of water and placed it next to my bed. I was fascinated by this young man's kindness. I drank the water and watched him go back to sleep, completely covering himself under his blanket. By now I was feeling exhausted after my journey and yet unable to lay my head down. I looked in awe at the Bedouin family, sound asleep on the rooftop, and I looked at my black Sabbath shoes, once clean and polished but now dusty and unrecognizable. I tried to understand what I had done but a deep tiredness came over me. I covered myself with the blanket but lay trembling on the mattress as beads of sweat ran down my back in the cold desert night. At five o'clock Jasser rose and covered me with his blanket, and only then did I fall asleep.

After the morning milking, at about seven o'clock, Taisir, one of Suleiman's sons, came to wake me up.

"Get up!" he said, shaking me with two hands.

"Oh no, I'm so tired!" I pleaded, peering from under my blankets.

His eyes, however, opened wide with an angry look.

"My father is waiting – you must come *quickly*!"

Taisir handed me a jug of water and pointed to a place over the hill where I could wash.

"*Hurry!*" he shouted.

Engraved on my mind was the moon's silver light that touched the surrounding hilltops in the night. The morning, however, was painted in rich, earthy colours of browns and taupe greys, and the sky was a sparkling blue. I found a private spot to wash where tiny blades of grass glistened between the wet pebbles, still wet from an early morning dew. I washed my face as best I could and hurried back, but along the way I stopped to admire the sun rising from behind the hilltops, kindling the tall palm trees with the warm light of morning.

"*Hurry up!*" Taisir shouted impatiently, pushing me into the old pumping station.

Suleiman and Jasser were seated on the floor, waiting to eat breakfast. Suleiman signalled for me to sit down with them, and then he blessed the food in the way that Muslims do — but I did not bless. The three of us ate from one platter of goat's cheese with olive oil and freshly made bread, but we ate in silence.

After we finished, Fatimah entered the room with a pot of tea, and she wished me good morning with a smile. She took away the empty platter, but Suleiman and Jasser sat there with morbid faces, not saying a word. Only then did it occur to me that Suleiman was waiting for me to give him an explanation as to why I had come in the middle of the night. I told him that I had to get away from the festival of *Sukkot* — but this did not impress him. They both continued sitting with the same sullen look, but then Suleiman spoke.

"You are foolish!" he barked angrily; "you could have fallen down the ravine, or have been eaten by wolves, or you could have been beaten by thieves – *or murdered!*"

I was shocked. I had not expected to be reprimanded and felt my ears burning with shame. I recalled the four Jewish boys who had been murdered in Wadi Kelt, and my heart began to beat faster as I imagined what could have happened to me in the middle of night. I looked at Jasser with his head bowed, but they both continued sitting in silence.

Then Suleiman burst out laughing. "You're like a Bedouin!" he exclaimed, loudly.

Then Jasser laughed out loud too and Suleiman clapped his hands with delight. He said that I was to spend the day grazing with Jasser, and he whistled to Taisir to open the gates of the pen where the goats were waiting impatiently.

The goats charged out of the pen but Suleiman's children, eager to do their part, directed them over to the other side of the *wadi* whilst running jubilantly on stones and over rocks. It was a wonderful sight, and it appeared to me that even the goats were jubilant, with smiles on their faces too!

Jasser jumped onto his donkey, but as he galloped off he quickly confirmed with his mother that she had packed extra food and water for me too, and then called out to me to follow him — and he was gone. I ran down into the *wadi*, through the dry river bed, and ascended the other side, trying to catch up with the herd. Jasser was way ahead of me but I climbed over the aqueduct, and up the other side of the *wadi*, ascending the mountainside, and I finally caught up with the herd. Jasser was leading the herd, sitting comfortably on his donkey, singing Bedouin love songs with great gusto.

Jasser noticed that I was out of breath and promptly jumped off his donkey insisting that I ride. I mounted the donkey, wrapping my legs tightly around, and I could feel the donkey's muscles ripple beneath me as he climbed the steep mountainside. His large head swayed from side to side, he blew through his nostrils, and occasionally he threw his head back with a loud snort. His name was Ahwah, and I patted him on the neck in gratitude. When I needed him to go faster I squeezed him with my legs; it was as if I was pressing on the accelerator.

I glanced towards the Bedouin encampment in the distance, now a small oasis in the vast desert, and gave a triumphant smile as I ascended the mountainside. As we climbed the mountain I listened to the sounds: the tinkling of bells, and the coughing and farting of the herd, and I could feel the hot desert wind blowing particles of sand against the skin of my face.

Jasser was a tough young man, born and bred in the *wadi*, and he knew of no other life. There was something very appealing about his ruggedness; he was dark skinned with black, closely-set eyes, a large mouth and strong cheek bones. He was of a lean build with powerful muscles, his bushy eyebrows met in the middle, and he had a moustache. He did not speak Hebrew, and I knew very little Arabic, and yet we managed to understand each other very well. He had a *Joie de vivre* and I laughed a lot when with him.

We made it to the top and I dismounted the donkey. To the east was a view of the Moab mountain range with the Dead Sea in the foreground, but to the west the land was parched dry with no sign of civilization whatsoever: only dust. I asked Jasser where the goats graze because there was no pasture land in sight, but he showed me the abundance of dried thistles all over the land and extracted a few seeds and ate them with a grin. But then I inquired as to where the goats drink. He took out the water supply for us to drink and pointed westwards, in the direction that we were heading, and indicated that we must continue. We marched on in the extreme heat but there was still nothing in sight except the distant horizon. Occasionally Jasser mounted Ahwah and galloped off to encircle the herd and keep them intact, and as I watched him, it occurred to me that he could be the soul of one of the seven shepherds of Israel.

Noticing that I was apparently red from the sun, Jasser covered my head with a *Keffiyeh* scarf and instructed me to roll down my shirt sleeves. We continued walking overland until finally, in the distance, a lone tree came into view and the goats began to lead the way, gathering momentum as they headed towards the tree.

Next to the tree was a well, preserved by Arabs from the city of Ramallah for the Bedouins to water their flocks. Jasser opened the heavy metal door that covered the mouth of the well and, taking out a bucket, tied a rope and lowered it into the well. He drew buckets of water from the well and filled rows of troughs adjacent to the well, but the goats clambered over each other to get to the troughs. Suddenly Jasser yelled at them loudly, and they stopped immediately, just like obedient house pets.

After Jasser had watered the goats they wandered over to the tree to rest. We unpacked the supplies, and while Jasser prepared a pot of tea I collected dry wood for the fire. We then sat cross-legged opposite each other, with an old sack-cloth as our tablecloth, and ate a meal of boiled potatoes, olive oil and bread, prepared by his mother Fatimah in the morning. When the tea boiled, Jasser added a sprig of wild thyme and let it brew while we ate the tastiest meal I had ever eaten. I wiped my tin plate clean with the bread and drank glass after glass of hot, sweet tea with a delightful herbal scent.

Afterwards we both felt very tired and lay down to sleep with the goats under the tree.

On the journey back the goats raced to get home; apparently they knew that food awaited them there. Jasser galloped around the herd, keeping them intact, and prevented them from running forward in the direction of home. The closer we came to base the more difficult it became.

We stopped half way for a rest and while Jasser was busy rounding up the goats, I prepared a fire for another pot of tea. Jasser, however, was particular about the ritual of tea-making and would not let me make the tea. According to him, Bedouin tea had to have exactly the right amount of tea leaves and exactly the right amount of sugar, and he considered it a task that only a Bedouin could do!

We drank the delicious tea, but before I could finish Jasser was up and off on his donkey, rounding up the herd as they moved rapidly back towards base.

I packed up and caught up with them at the aqueduct, where the goats were drinking. Jasser and I took a dip in the aqueduct and refreshed ourselves in the cold water. Suddenly, and quite unexpectedly, while the goats were still drinking, Jasser jumped on his donkey and galloped off down into the *wadi*, while still completely wet.

With Jasser down at the bottom of the *wadi*, the herd then made their descent but stopped abruptly in front of the place where Jasser stood: three hundred goats kept their eyes fixed on Jasser, waiting for his signal to go.

In the meantime Jasser's brothers and sisters were filling the troughs with grain for the herd to eat.

And then Jasser gave the signal.

The herd rushed towards the troughs and a great cloud of dust rose up to the skies. For a moment it appeared to me that they were stampeding, but the goats emerged from the cloud of dust in rich colours of browns and black, clambering for a place at the troughs. Within moments they were eating in contentment while the red glow of sunset filtered through the cloud of dust.

As the dust settled, the goats were led to the pen where Suleiman, with his two wives, started the evening milking.

Nightfall fell upon Wadi Kelt and I was saddened that I would have to leave. Joel would be coming to meet me at the top of the *wadi* when *Sukkot* ended at sundown. Before I left I called out to Suleiman to thank him for everything, but he stopped milking and came over to me.

"Yonatan, you must stay to eat with us!" he said.

I explained to him that Joel would be waiting but asked if I could return another time. He answered that I was welcome to stay with them next time and we shook hands. I started the steep climb up and out of the *wadi*, waving to Suleiman's family while they helped with the milking. They all waved back, and it was a beautiful sight for me to see.

Joel was waiting for me at the top of the *wadi* and I smiled upon seeing him. I had feared that he would be angry but instead he was interested in having an account of my day. I proceeded to tell him all about my experience, and even as we entered his house I was still talking enthusiastically about it.

Nomi asked: "Did you eat?"

"Yes, thank you, of course I ate!" I replied.

"But you didn't eat in a *Sukkah*," she answered, coldly.

It was true. There was not a *Sukkah* in the desert, but I had experienced the *life* of the desert, the cold of night, and the heat of noon. I sampled life like the shepherds of Israel had once lived, and I experienced true hospitality. I felt that my day had been more authentic that dwelling in a ready-made temporary hut with coloured paper chains from Mea Shearim.

The life of the Bedouins was how I imagined Jews had lived in Biblical times. I was fascinated by the Bedouin people and their culture, and I did not want to lose the positive energy that I felt after my day. I decided to go home right away, but as I was leaving Joel asked me to enter his *Sukkah* and make the necessary blessing on the Four Plants. I had no problem with that and did it for him.

Chapter 16
The Intermediate days

The intermediate days of the week of *Sukkot* are a semi-holiday and from my apartment window I could hear my neighbours celebrating in their temporary huts outside. I watched them as they walked to synagogue with the Four Plants, and I felt that I did not belong in that world anymore. I wanted to run away and be free of the obligation to perform the rituals.

In a few days it would be *Hoshanah Rabbah* – the day of the willow – and the last chance to be forgiven for one's sins. Then, on the last day of *Sukkot*, it would be *Simchat Torah* – the Rejoicing of the Torah – which is the most joyous day in the year. On this day, to mark the beginning of the annual Torah reading in synagogue, the worshipers dance with the Torah scrolls throughout the streets of Jerusalem.

I was determined not to be at home for the last days of the festival: I had to get away!

I arranged to take vacation days and left the office at noon, smiling at the hot winds beckoning me to come to the desert. There was still no rain but, although the days were getting cooler, there were days that were extremely hot and dry; the sudden changes were typical for that time of the year, and are known as the *Khamsin*, a hot desert wind that blows in from the Arabian Desert.

First of all I drove home to change out of my airline uniform and packed. I threw a full duffel bag into my estate car and drove through Jabel Mukaber, the Arab neighbourhood below the hill from where I had painted my watercolours of Jerusalem. On a regular day I was able to see as far as the Dead Sea but on this day, due to the *Khamsin*, there was just a yellow haze.

I continued down the winding road, through the Kidron Valley, into Silwan, and past crowded Arab neighbourhoods built into the hillsides. The diffused yellow light, reflecting gently upon the whitewashed houses, cast murky shadows, but when driving up the steep hill on the other side of the valley, the magnificent Dome of the Rock shrine suddenly dominated my view. There I took a sharp right-turn and drove through Bethany and al-Eizariya.

All along the roadside in al-Eizariya, boxes of fresh vegetables were laid out in a dramatic display of colour. There were endless rows of boxes filled with bright-red chili peppers, light-green peppers, and bunches of carrots with their stems and leaves. There were purple aubergines, dark green courgettes, cucumbers, and huge boxes of ripe tomatoes. The vibrant colours and fresh vegetables were inviting and therefore I stopped my car to buy some vegetables only to discover that they were sold by the box. So I loaded up the estate car with boxes of vegetables!

I continued driving on, with my estate car now full of boxes, past Maaleh-Adumim where Joel and Naomi lived, down the steep highway that cuts through the hills (those same hills which I had walked down on the first night of *Sukkot*), descending through the desert, past Bedouin encampments along the way, and finally turned off at Mitzpe Yericho. Here I found the dirt path that leads down to Wadi Kelt. I drove my car down at a very slow pace, carefully avoiding the rocks and hollows, all the way to the bottom of the *wadi,* where I parked my car. I turned off the ignition and listened to the silence.

There was not a sound in the *wadi* except the bleating of a distant goat. I looked across the *wadi* but nothing stirred; the flourmill, the tall palm trees, and the parched riverbed remained still in the heat of the *Khamsin.*

The Bedouins awoke from their siesta and Suleiman wandered over to me, seemingly half asleep. We shook hands but upon seeing the boxes of vegetables in my estate car, his face lit up and he laughed with joy. He ordered his sons to carry the boxes inside, and then he ordered his wives to start cooking.

We sat down on a mattress while Suleiman took his time – as is the way of the Bedouin – calmly rolling a cigarette, and lighting it. As he drew the cigarette smoke into his mouth and lungs, it seemed that it had the distinct smell of marijuana. According to Suleiman, however, it was Bedouin Tobacco, apparently produced from a shrub that grows down in the *wadi*. He appeared very happy when smoking it, but I was inclined to think that he was genuinely pleased to see me *and* the boxes of vegetables.

While tea was being served we discussed my sleeping arrangements. I told him that I planned to stay in the nearby cave, and Suleiman listened attentively. He reminisced about the time when it was used as a pen for the goats in the days when they had first come to live in Wadi Kelt, but then he looked up to the skies with a disapproving look and warned me that there would be rain. I imagined myself alone in the cave and was delighted at the thought of rain falling outside! I suspected, however, that Suleiman did not approve of my idea. As we drank our tea, Suleiman sipped in silent contemplation and asked Taisir to go with me to inspect the cave.

After a somewhat difficult climb by way of a narrow ridge in the rock formation, we reached the entrance to the cave. To my surprise it was larger inside than I had anticipated and it had a remarkable view over the *wadi*. I was captivated. Taisir, however, inspected the walls and said that I could not stay there. I laughed at his blasé manner, but he took a stone and drew two pictures on the cave-wall, one of a snake, and one of a scorpion. This made me laugh even more. I wondered where the snakes and scorpions were, but Taisir was most adamant about it. And yet, he had a mischievous look about him and stood there with his hand on his hip looking very smug. He was a handsome young man, extremely thin, with large brown eyes and a serious look about him, but as we walked back he had a perpetual grin on his face which baffled me.

When Taisir reported to his father that there were snakes and scorpions, Suleiman seemed extremely concerned. But then he roared with laughter. He said that it was a stupid idea to think that I could live in a cave and told me that I would sleep on the roof of the pumping station with the rest of his family.

That evening I ate zucchinis stuffed with rice that had been cooked in goat's yogurt. The flavour was exceedingly strong, like the intense smell of goats, but I eventually acquired a taste for it. Suleiman explained that the strong flavour was because the goats graze outside in pasture the whole year-round. He showed me the hard white-rock substance which was yogurt, dried in the sun and kept the whole year without refrigeration.

When I went to bed on the roof I could not sleep for most of the night; the mosquitos were on my eyes, up my nose and in my ears. I looked over at Jasser who slept soundly under his blanket, and I buried myself under my blanket but almost suffocated. There were other disturbances too. The boys kept getting up, and from under my blanket I peeped at them standing on the edge of the roof for no apparent reason. I was baffled as to what they were doing, just standing there in the middle of the night. I even heard a strange hammering noise, a sort of sustained sound like a drum roll. Then I solved the mystery. They were urinating from the roof top, and it was the heavy stream of urine hitting the dusty earth below that made the drumming sound.

In the early hours of the morning, when I finally did begin to fall asleep, I was awoken by Suleiman's first wife, Fatimah, getting up to make bread and to prepare a large kettle of tea. It fascinated me how Suleiman shared his wives and with whom he slept the previous night. But it also intrigued me to know how it must have felt for Fatimah, in the prime of her life, when he brought home another woman to live with them.

After making the bread, Fatimah woke up the children to get them ready for school. She dressed them in clean clothes, wetted and combed their hair, and sat them down to a breakfast of fresh bread and olive oil. Afterwards they climbed upon their donkeys and rode up and out of the *wadi* to the main road, where they took taxis to the UNWRA School in the Aqabat-Jaber refugee camp, in Jericho.

I got up and went into the hills to answer the call of nature; luckily Jasser had taught me to use three stones to wipe. The older boys got up to pray, and then they helped with the morning milking. After the milking was finished there was a second sitting for breakfast. We ate fresh cheese, fresh bread, and fresh olive oil with a strong and bitter taste, and we drank lots of sweet tea.

After breakfast Jasser and I went out with the goats. Visibility was bad due to the *Khamsin*, and as we ascended the mountainside I noticed the view back towards the pumping station was like an old black and white photograph in sepia tones. Particles of sand ground between my teeth, my eyelids felt rough, and my face was tight as particles of dust caked to my skin. Jasser gave me the *Keffiyeh* to mask my face, leaving only my eyes open to the weather, but the journey was nonetheless strenuous; we choked on the dust, and we could hardly speak as we trekked towards the well with the grains of sand blinding our view.

Happily, by the time that we arrived at the well there were signs that the *Khamsin* was subsiding. Jasser opened the heavy metal door and filled the troughs with water, and as the goats clambered over each other to drink he made his ablutions and prayed towards Mecca.

After we had prepared tea, we sat down to eat and I asked Jasser why he prayed but had not prayed the last time that we were at the well. The reason, he told me, was because he was not clean then. We struggled with the language, but he used the word "*taharah*" for clean, which is the same word used in the Jewish religion meaning purity, a term not used for physical cleanliness but rather to describe a spiritual state of being. This helped me understand the Muslim concept of clean.

I asked him why he had not made the ablutions to be pure the last time we were at the well. He told me that last time he had masturbated, and that after the ejaculation of semen one is not clean, meaning that he was not in a state of ritual purity and therefore needed to make a full ablution. This time, however, he was clean, but he still needed a partial ablution to remove any possible trace of urine and excrement. He explained that the partial ablution was required after going to the toilet, or even if one breaks wind, and we both laughed when I learnt the Arabic word for fart.

Later that evening, the women and small children ate separately. The males sat cross-legged around one large platter and I learnt that each one eats from his segment of the platter only. The custom is to honour the guest by putting the best from their segment of the platter, onto the guest's segment.

After the meal they brought soap and water to wash, for we had eaten with our hands, and they never allowed my glass of tea to remain empty. The floor was brushed clean and then we sat around in a circle. All the small children fought to sit next to me, caressing my arms and stroking my hair, and more tea was served. The purpose of sitting this way was so that everybody could talk about their day, or about any other topic that they wished to talk about.

It appeared as if they were storytelling; they improvised, with gestures and expressions, to make it more entertaining, and the audience listened intently with their eyes glued on the narrator. I did not understand most of what was said but even so it was a pleasure to live intimately with them, and before long I forgot my fantasy of living alone in a cave.

Suleiman's prophesy of rain came true and on the third night the skies opened up; huge drops of rain began to fall upon us while in our beds on the roof. Everybody jumped up and grabbed their mattresses and blankets, and we ran downstairs into the building. It was crowded inside but we arranged our mattresses, and in a short while everyone was fast asleep again. I lay awake watching the flashes of lightning that lit up the strange room, and then I waited for the claps of thunder.

Early in the morning I had to get up with all the brothers so that they could lay out their prayer mats and prepare the room for prayers. I sat in the corner watching them pray, pure and clean after their ablutions, with one of the brothers leading the Dawn Prayer, and the others in a line behind him. I watched them with pain in my heart; it seemed odd that they were praying to the one God, but I sat there indifferently and ignored Him.

The morning was bright and clear after the heavy rains with an unusual transparency in the air. The land was washed of dust, and the foliage in the *wadi* appeared enhanced; jumping out in spectacular tones of green against the drenched ochre coloured mountains. The palm leaves sparkled with raindrops of emerald green, and the long and sensuous trunks, wet and intensely brown, cut across the view of the majestic flourmill now seeped in tones of burnt sienna.

The crisp air was filled with a bouquet of herbs as I crossed over the river bed, flowing with water. I listened to the birds' song echoing down the *wadi*, the goats jumped merrily, bleating jubilantly at the discovery of a new world, and their coats gave out a heavy musk fragrance. I mounted *Ahwah* the donkey and ascended the mountainside with a feeling of contentment and smiled at the oasis below me; I could see Suleiman's children in the distance, running naked outside the white walls of the pumping station. Jasser marched by my side, deep in thought. When we reached the top, he took Ahwah to round up the herd and we continued westward bound.

As I walked over the land, I felt the ground soft and damp, now with a spring to it after the rains. I strolled among the herd and made a new friend with a nannie-goat; she nibbled at my fingers and I stopped to admire her pretty little face. I stroked her white beard and played with her comical wattles that dangled from her neck. When she ate the seeds from my hand, Jasser laughed in bewilderment. Her name was Samour and she followed me everywhere.

We came to the well, and after Jasser had finished watering the goats I observed them as they wandered over to the tree like a group of elegant ladies at a social event; they found their lady friends and sat down to gossip.

Jasser made his ablutions to pray the Noon Prayer while I prepared a fire from dry firewood that we had packed among our supplies.

I was fascinated while watching Jasser pray, and I set my eyes upon him. I recalled what he had told me about the ablutions and *taharah* in respect to a man having to be pure and clean to pray. His words had impressed me a lot. Ever since I had stopped praying, on the first day of the festival of *Sukkot*, I had been feeling withdrawal symptoms. Now I had a craving to pray each time that I saw Jasser praying.

After the Noon Prayer Jasser attended to his customary ritual of tea making and left the kettle to cook on the smouldering cinders. The sun came out from behind the clouds, warming our backs, as we set out our food on the old sack cloth. Suddenly the tin lid blew off, and the tea boiled over, creating a strange aroma of burnt sugar and tea, and a cloud of smoke erupted from the fire like a volcanic eruption. We ate a delicious meal of goat's cheese, olives, and olive oil with bread, and Jasser saved the olive pits for a game of marbles. After drinking Jasser's strong, sweet tea, we both fell asleep in the warmth of the afternoon sun.

But we were awoken by the restless goats and quickly prepared ourselves for the journey back. Jasser threw the saddle over Ahwah the donkey and filled the saddle pockets with the remaining supplies, arranging everything neatly; he was very proud of his saddle made from old sacks because he had sewn it himself, in a somewhat coarse fashion using a large needle and string. He galloped off to round up the herd, and I walked on in contentment, enjoying the warm afternoon sun. I eventually caught up with them and joined the herd, enjoying the serenity of being with the flock of goats and listening to them chewing the cud. Samour the nannie goat came over to nibble at my fingers.

On the way back we stopped for another tea-break, and while the tea was cooking Jasser made his ablutions for the Afternoon Prayer. Before Jasser stood to pray, however, I asked him if I may stand next to him. He considered this for a moment and agreed. The clouds had completely disappeared and visibility was clear as we stood, looking over the Dead Sea, beyond the Hashemite Kingdom of Jordan, and in the direction of Mecca, Saudi Arabia. I listened to Jasser uttering the holy words, I bowed down with him, and I went through the motions with him.

When we arrived back to the old pumping station Jasser told his mother, and she in turn told Suleiman, who came to ask me if it was true. At first he was harsh when speaking to me due to his concern that one must be pure when praying to God; a full ablution was necessary when praying, but I was not a Muslim. He was not learned enough to know, and therefore he went to discuss the matter with Fatimah.

In the meantime they prayed the Sunset Prayer, but I was not invited to pray with them.

After the evening meal, while drinking our tea, Suleiman announced that he would take me in the morning to the Mosque in Jericho to discuss the matter with the Sheikh. He then invited me to join them for the Evening Prayer.

The next morning at the mosque in Jericho, the Sheikh arranged for a practicing Muslim to show me how to make the full ablution. This was done downstairs, below the mosque's prayer hall, where there were facilities for washing and showering. He then gave me some perfumed oil and we went upstairs to the prayer hall where he showed me how to pray.

With two witnesses present, I made the declaration in Arabic for the intention of converting to Islam:

> *"I bear witness that there is no god except Allah.*
> *And I bear witness that Muhammad is Allah's messenger.*
> *And I bear witness that Jesus is the slave and messenger of Allah.*
> *I deny and refuse any religion except Islam."*

The Sheikh recited a few more prayers, and I was astonished how easy it was to become a Muslim.

Chapter 17
Yunus

Sitting under the papaya tree in Ahmad's *bustan*, I breathed in the exotic fragrances of several kinds of fruit trees, some of which I had never seen before: mango trees, guava trees, kumquat trees, and vines of passion-fruit that dressed the walls in glorious shades of purple and green.

Most of the year round Jericho is hot and dry, but the air in Ahmad's *bustan* was moist due to the constant irrigating and washing. Ahmad syphoned water from the aqueduct which brought the water supply from Jerusalem to Jericho, and he splashed water over the foliage at least three times a day. The *bustan* was a tropical garden with sweet perfumes that filled the air.

There was a loud, amplified call to prayer coming from the local minaret, and then the haunting sound as the call to prayer was repeated, like an echo, from the minarets all around Jericho:

Allahu Akbar – Allahu Akbar – Allahu Akbar – Allahu Akbar.

"Yunus!" said Ahmad, calling from the *madafa*. "Make your ablutions and let's go and pray!"

Ahmad gave me the name Yunus, after the Prophet Yunus — who is Jonah in the Bible — and occasionally he called me Yunus Njoom, after the name of his tribe, because I was now considered a brother. As we hurried to the mosque, Ahmad's long white *Gallabiyah* blew in the desert breeze against the contour of his slim build; I saw the bulge of his manhood and my heart jumped a beat. There was no doubt, however, that I admired Ahmad because he was a pious Muslim, and my relationship with him was pure.

Ahmad repeated the words with the muezzin:

Allah is the Greatest — I bear witness that there is no god but Allah — I bear witness that Muhammad is Allah's messenger.

We took off our shoes before entering the mosque and joined the rows of Muslims as it was announced that prayers had begun. I stood beside Ahmad in prayer and could smell the fragrance of musk upon him.

I recall the anxiety attacks I used to have when entering a synagogue; I sat in fear of being called-up to participate in religious duties on the *bimah*, the small stage where the Torah scroll was read and where the blessings were made, and if I was called-up to the *bimah* my heart would thump against my chest. I could hardly recite the words of the blessings, and I would feel my face turning red knowing that I was being watched and judged by the congregation. I hated going to synagogue.

But now I felt confident in a mosque, where we all stood equal in prayer.

Indeed, I entered my new world without fear, travelling freely throughout the Palestinian Territories, where I stopped to pray in different mosques along the way. I enjoyed praying with other Muslims and made new friends. The congregants, detecting that I was not a local Arab, were inquisitive, and upon learning that I had converted to Islam, they loved me; but they loved me even more when they learnt that I had been a Christian *and* a Jew. They preached the basic beliefs of Islam: that the Jews and Christians had distorted their holy books, but the Holy Qur'an was sent down to Muhammad (peace be upon him) in its original form, unchanged and undistorted, and that it was the last Book. They invited me to their homes to talk about Islam, and to eat and to pray with them. Islam penetrated into every aspect of my life, and deep into my soul.

In the past I had observed the forty days of Lent, and I had fasted on *Yom Kippur* and on other fast days too, but none came near to the ecstatic feeling I felt when fasting for the entire month of *Ramadan*.

I rose each morning for the ablutions and pre-dawn meal and conquered hunger and thirst from dawn to dusk. I emptied myself of negative thoughts, and sexual desires, and cleansed myself of sin. I experienced an extraordinary awareness of God that I had not known before, and I wished that the fast of *Ramadan* would not end. I wanted to live in complete submission to God, always.

After the month of *Ramadan* ended, when the month of *Shawwal* was announced with the sighting of the new moon, we celebrated *Eid al-Fitr* – the breaking of the fast – with prayers of thanksgiving.

After the month of *Shawwal* came the month of *Dhu al-Qa'dah*, and then, on the tenth of the month of *Dhu al-Hijjah*, in the time of the *Hajj* pilgrimage to Mecca, we celebrated *Eid al-Adha* – the Festival of the Sacrifice. It commemorates Abraham's willingness to sacrifice his son Ishmael.

I confess that I was mystified by the Muslim belief that it was Ishmael and not Isaac whom Abraham was told to sacrifice. And yet, after studying the text in the Hebrew Bible about the Sacrifice of Isaac, in which God refers to Isaac as Abraham's *only* son when in fact he already had a son named Ishmael, I began to see what could be the distortions in the Bible that the Muslims were referring to.

And yet again, I was not convinced. I found the contradiction very troubling, but I had to believe it because I was now a Muslim named Yunus.

Chapter 18
Khadra

On one of my visits to Wadi Kelt I could hear the laughter of Bedouin children as I drove down into the *wadi.* They came running towards me, chanting: *"Yunus... Yunus...Yunus!"*

The Bedouin children were always happy; they were thrilled when playing a game of marbles made from pellets of goat's dung, they were ecstatic when eating the shards of cauliflower that their mother had discarded, and they were delighted when running barefoot in the dirt. On this particular day they had a special reason to be happy: their aunt Khadra had come to stay with her herd of goats!

Khadra was Suleiman's divorced sister and was regarded by some – including Suleiman – as one who brought shame on the family. Their father had arranged the marriage, but she walked out on the abusive husband and his scheming first wife who could not contain her jealousy. Both the husband and the first wife made Khadra's life very unpleasant, and so she fled from their harsh treatment and went into hiding. Only after she was able to secure a divorce did she return to the clan and to her father's house. She then became a shepherdess, and in certain months of the year she brought the herd to Wadi Kelt to graze.

In keeping with the Islamic dress code, she covered her hair and wore layers of clothing. She wore tweed, apparently suitable for its durability and the outside lifestyle, and yet it made her appear elegant and refined as she galloped through dry river-beds and up the mountainsides.

I watched her curiously as she laughed gaily with the children and carried out her daily chores with Suleiman's wives.

"Yunus, I'm going to make tea!" she said, in her gentle voice.

When she poured the tea, she whispered my name, "Yunus!"

My heart beat quickly from her charming manner, and the way she spoke so softly and kindly. I did not know that I was capable of feelings for a girl, and yet I felt attracted to Khadra. Alas, Suleiman glared at me with beady eyes, and his wives watched my every move.

Therefore I waited for another occasion and came in search of her.

I left my car on the old Roman road to Jericho and walked along the ridge overlooking the *wadi* until I could see a herd of goats. When I was sure that it was Khadra's herd, I made my descent. The goats grazed on the sides of the cliff, but Khadra had tied up her donkey and found a cave to rest in. She saw me and called out to me, and I saw her radiant smile. She gave me directions how to descend the steep cliff but I was not familiar with the terrain, and I got stuck on the cliff-side. I froze and was unable to move; unable to descend, and unable to ascend, from the fear of falling. There was a sheer drop down into the ravine below, and it was very dangerous.

Khadra cried, not knowing what to do or how to help me, but I let my body slide down onto the narrow ledge below me, while still clinging onto the upper ledge, and prayed that I would not fall to my death. At last I felt my feet touch the narrow ledge below and somehow managed to manoeuvre myself sideways into the cave.

She had tears in her eyes and pleaded with me never to do it again. Indeed, I was deeply shaken, but Khadra promised that next time she would come to me.

The next time that I came, Khadra was nowhere to be seen, and so I made my descent to the pastures below, next to St. George's Monastery. I walked through the grass, lush and green from the waters of the aqueduct, and I sang a Psalm of David:

The Lord is my shepherd, I shall not want; He makes me lie down in green pastures.

He leads me beside still waters; He restores my soul.

He leads me in paths of righteousness for His name's sake.

Even though I walk through the valley of the shadow of death, I fear no evil; for Thou art with me; Thy rod and Thy staff, they comfort me.

Thou preparest a table before me in the presence of my enemies; Thou anointest my head with oil, my cup overflows.

Surely goodness and mercy shall follow me all the days of my life; and I shall dwell in the House of the Lord – forever.

I looked up to the cliffs on both sides of the valley, to the narrow ledges, caves and crevices, where I could have fallen to my death. The sound of vultures echoed down the valley, and it seemed that I was indeed walking *through the valley of the shadow of death.*

I began to have a feeling that I was walking the wrong path in life. I felt pangs of melancholy, and I felt fear. I did not feel comfort.

The monastery soared above the valley, the white walls reflected the midday sun, and the turquoise domes and red-roofed verandas glistened over the valley. I climbed all the way up to the aqueduct and rested there for a while, watching the water plunge down to the green pastures below.

I then followed the aqueduct upstream in anticipation of finding Khadra.

In the quiet of the *wadi*, I listened to the gentle sound of water flowing down towards Jericho. The calming of the waters led me to reflect upon my life.

I wondered if I were to marry Khadra, whether I would be capable of being with her. I loved her soul, but in my heart of hearts I knew that I was incapable of being with a woman. And yet I continued to pursue her, caught up in a world of hope and make-believe.

At last I saw her from afar, as she and the herd moved up the *wadi* in the direction of the flourmill. The air stood still deep down in the *wadi*, where sound seemed subdued except for the buzzing of an occasional fly, but in the distance I could hear the faint chime of tin bells and the bleating of goats. High above, beyond the walls of the *wadi*, the vultures circled silently against a blue sky.

I finally caught up and blended in with the flow of the herd, and I listened to the sounds; the goats chewing, the tin bells, and the herd moving through the dry grass. It occurred to me that the Psalms of David must have been inspired in those same surroundings. Khadra, feeling my presence, turned her gaze on me and whispered, "Yunus" in the voice of an angel. She smiled as I walked in silence, and with a mutual understanding that we do not come physically close. In the afternoon light I caught a glimpse of her as her scarf fell, revealing her long hair. I should have turned my head, but I could not take my eyes off from her. She was handsome, her skin was weathered and lined from the hot desert winds, and her long black hair, which had strands of grey, was parted down the middle.

As she gathered her hair up and twisted it into a bun, I was able to see her beauty for the first time, but then she tied her scarf tightly around her head, in the Muslim way. Her face was round with small, dark eyes set deeply in their sockets, and her cheekbones protruded. The afternoon light shone upon her white scarf which contrasted with her dark and weather-beaten skin, and I was reminded of an African ceremonial mask.

Khadra did not wear perfume but as she walked before me, I sensed that she had the smell of goats and of smoking wood-fires. I loved her smell, but suddenly she stopped in her tracks. I thought that she had seen a snake, but her hearing was sharp and I had not heard Suleiman who was shouting from across the *wadi*.

"*Who do you think you are?*" Suleiman yelled. "Do you think you are a foreign woman? Get out from there immediately!"

Khadra turned to me with a look of horror in her eyes.

"Yunus, Suleiman is very angry. You must go right away!" she cried as she mounted her donkey.

I continued up the *wadi* but I was concerned; I knew that I had done something wrong coming to speak with Khadra. I continued up river and avoided going to the old pumping station, on Suleiman's side of the *wadi*.

I headed to the flourmill, on the other side of the *wadi*, and found Helwa sitting outside on a chair. Muhammad Abu Abdullah had passed away, leaving his second wife Helwa and her children alone in the flourmill. Helwa was getting on in years and the harsh life in the *wadi* had taken its toll. She was a chain-smoker, and she had diabetes, and she was therefore not in the best of health. She held a cigarette between her thin, dark and wrinkled fingers and in the other hand, that rested on her lap, she clung to a packet of filtered cigarettes. She wore a black Bedouin dress that was hand embroidered in cross-stitches of red, and her hair was covered in a plain black scarf wrapped around her dark, wrinkled face and neck. Her dark watery eyes were lined with *kohl* and her eyelids hung with excess skin, her cheeks were hollow and she was now toothless.

Her daughter-in-law, Hanya, came to welcome me: "Yunus, *Aassalamu Alaikum*, come and drink!"

Hanya was married to Helwa's eldest son, Atta, who was now considered head of the flourmill since the passing of his father. I had arrived by way of the aqueduct that runs adjacent to the top floor of the flourmill, where they sat outside. The three of us chatted about nothing of great importance but I observed them both. Helwa chain-smoked, used her finished cigarette to light yet another cigarette, and Hanya chatted vivaciously while washing the tea glasses in the aqueduct. I recalled how, in the past, she had spoken to me in the Hebrew language, but now she spoke to me only in Arabic.

The fire was smouldering and Hanya filled the burnt, black kettle with filtered water from a Jerrycan, and placed it onto the hot cinders. She added some twigs and leant down, blowing gently onto the smouldering coals, until a flame was produced. I noticed that she wore a grubby red dress but with a chain of solid gold coins around her neck. Streaks of dirt ran down her hot face, reddened by the burning fire, and she wiped the sweat from her brow. She wore a colourful scarf that fell to her shoulders and did not care to cover her curly black hair, but continued chatting to me.

I sat cross-legged on a mattress, still observing Helwa and Hanya, with the desert hills behind their silhouettes. Hanya poured the tea and went about her chores while Helwa sat peeling potatoes with a cigarette in her mouth. My thoughts, however, were with Khadra. I was infatuated with her and wanted to marry her.

I went for a walk in the direction of the waterfall where I could make my ablutions, and along the way I noticed the last remnants of water in the *wadi*. The *wadi* was dry almost all year round, except after the rainy season, but now it would be dry again for another year.

When I came to the waterfall I sat on the rock to rest before making my ablutions. The rock was still warm from the sun, and so I lay down with the heat of the rock warming my back. I listened to the sound of the waterfall plunging into the pool, but I fell into a deep sleep. When I awoke it took me a while to understand in which life I was living; I was confused, and only after some time did I realise that I was now Yunus. I quickly made my ablutions and ran back to the flourmill to pray.

As I prayed the Afternoon Prayer on the roof of the flourmill I heard Atta gallop in on his donkey. He had been out for the day with the herd but immediately, upon his arrival, commanded Hanya to go with him to their room. There was a small commotion, but she dropped everything and went with him.

Just as I was finishing my prayers, Atta's second wife Nura appeared. I completed my prayers and followed her down to the bottom level of the flourmill, where Atta's younger brother was milking the goats. I observed her as she joined him for the milking; she was pregnant and appeared massive in a traditional *jilbab,* a loose fitting outer garment that covered her entire body. It was a grey colour, and she wore a grey coloured scarf tied tightly around her head and neck. Her face was oval, and she had a very long nose and small eyes. I thought to myself how unattractive she looked now that she was married. I recalled the time when she was still single, when she lived in her father's house in the Aqabat-Jaber refugee camp in Jericho. She was tall and slim then, with long chestnut-brown hair, and she wore tight blue jeans and a cotton T-shirt without a bra.

Finally Atta came down to help with the milking, and greeted me jovially.

"*Assalamu Alaikum!*" he exclaimed, in the traditional words.

"*Wa Alaikum Assalam,*" I responded

Atta had a pitted and acned face and wore his *Keffiyeh* tied in a turban style. His stomach protruded excessively, stretching his white cotton *Gallabiyah*. He suddenly seemed very chirpy. He studied me closely with his beady eyes, and then he giggled in his usual way. I could not resist the temptation to ask him why, at such a young age, he needed two wives. His reply was that there was a lot of work that needed to be done in Wadi Kelt.

Suleiman called me from the other side of the *wadi* to come to eat with them, and so I said my farewells and headed across. I had hoped to see Khadra but she was intentionally kept from me and ate separately in another room with the women. I ate with the men in a friendly atmosphere, but I understood that the new arrangement was a polite way of telling me not to pursue Khadra anymore.

Chapter 19
Al-Aqsa Mosque

From my apartment in the Jewish neighbourhood of East Talpiot, I heard a familiar sound. It was a sound that I was accustomed to hearing in the past, but which meant nothing to me then. I listened to the *muezzin* in the neighbouring Arab village reciting the haunting and melodious *Adhan* – the call to prayer – but unlike in the past I now understood the meaning of every word.

I felt ecstatic and decided that I must go and pray in one of the mosques on the Arab side.

The picturesque Arab villages that surround East Talpiot always held a certain mystique for me and some of my watercolours reflect this. To the north of East Talpiot is Silwan, where little houses, domes and minarets climb out of the Kidron valley, up the slopes of the *Ophel* hillside, and meet the City of David just below the Old City of Jerusalem.

To the south of East Talpiot is Sur Baher, where clusters of old stone houses with arched-windows and verandas overlook the terraced olive groves below, and blend into the green hillside.

The call to prayer came from Sur Baher, opposite my apartment window, but there were a number of options where I could pray around East Talpiot. The most splendid of them was in the Al-Aqsa Mosque on *Al-Haram al-Sharif* – the Temple Mount – in the Old City of Jerusalem.

The first time that I prayed in the Al-Aqsa Mosque was in the month of Ramadan. My first impression, upon entering the *Al-Haram al-Sharif* compound, was the sheer beauty of the Dome of the Rock shrine; the outer octagonal shaped walls of white marble with porcelain tiles in stunning shades of greens and blues, the Islamic calligraphy, and the magnificent golden dome above. My next impression was the quiet as worshipers headed towards the Al-Aqsa Mosque. The *Al-Haram al-Sharif* is an enclosed area to where the worshipers come after having performed the ablutions for prayers, and they are in a state of purification.

The Qur'an says:

Surely Allah loves those who turn to Him constantly and He loves those who keep themselves pure and clean.

Those worshipers who need to re-new their ablutions stop to make a partial-ablution at the *Al-kas* fountain, a fountain encircled by ornate wrought-iron railings and surrounded by steps that lead down to tiny marble seats with individual taps.

I walked with the throng of worshipers, their voices low, with the muffled clatter of feet marching towards the grand entrance of the Al-Aqsa Mosque. The entrance was through a façade of massive stone arches, after which thousands of pairs of shoes were left outside before entering the huge and impressive interior of the glorious Al-Aqsa Mosque.

Upon entering in stockinged feet, the first thing I felt was the soft and plush carpet. I was overwhelmed by the vastness of the interior as my eyes were drawn up the massive, pure white marble columns, past geometric arches, and way up to the blue and gold painted ceiling. I stood in awe of the mosaics, calligraphy and stained-glass windows all around.

Some of the worshipers stopped to say a prayer upon entering the mosque and then joined the rows of worshipers for prayer. I sensed the sweet perfume of burning incense as I joined the rows of worshipers to pray, and I was overcome with a feeling of pride being in the Al-Aqsa Mosque.

With the *Iqamah* – the announcement that prayer has begun – thousands upon thousands of male worshipers, standing in rows, followed the Imam in prayer by reciting, in a whisper, utterances of Qur'anic verses while bowing, prostrating and sitting in unison from position to position. It generated a powerful meditation of soul and body-movement in worship of Allah. The religious experience of praying with the masses in the al-Aqsa Mosque was special, and all the more so in the month of Ramadan.

There was no doubt in my mind that the Muslims were worthy of their place on the Temple Mount. I could not comprehend how the Jews had come to such a low spiritual level and did not practice ritual purification; after all, it was the Jews who were required to be ritually clean to ascend the Temple. Why, I asked myself, were ablutions not required for Jews when praying?

I recalled that when praying with Jews, the only requirement was a mere rinse of the hands. How ironic, I thought, that I was standing on the Temple Mount *because* I was a Muslim! It made me shudder to think that Jews prayed after sexual relations with semen still upon them, after going to the toilet with urine and excrement on their body parts, and how they break wind when talking to God.

There were two security barriers before entering the *Al-Haram al-Sharif* enclosure. First, there was the Israeli security barrier, where I had to hide my Israeli identity but showed my British Passport with the name John Robert Screeton, passing as a British Muslim. I wore a *Keffiyeh* around my neck to help me look the part, but should they have checked on the computer it would have linked up to my Israeli identity and I would have been caught. I felt like a traitor but breathed a sigh of relief after the inspection, and then walked over to the second security barrier.

The second barrier was the Jerusalem Islamic Waqf security barrier, which was stricter. They were particularly suspicious of non-Muslims, especially since an Australian Christian tried to burn down the Al-Aqsa Mosque, and also a couple of Israeli Jews had once plotted to blow it up. Upon seeing my Anglo-Saxon features they stopped me right away. I showed them my British Passport, still hiding my Israeli Identity, but I was asked to recite the *Shahadah* – the declaration of faith – in Arabic. But that was not enough. I was also asked to recite the *Al-Fatiha* – the opening chapter of the Qur'an – but that was still not enough! They kept asking me to recite more and more verses from the Qur'an, and all of them had to be recited in the original Arabic.

This happened to me quite often when I went to pray at the Al-Aqsa Mosque. It seemed that they were suspicious and indeed, the Waqf security took me away to a room for questioning. I was irritated for being challenged as an authentic Muslim but they suspected me. They allowed me to pray in the room with a guard watching me, and then I was escorted out. That was the last straw. I never went to pray in the Al-Aqsa Mosque again.

In fact, I lived in fear of being caught on both sides. Yonatan Shaked was my official identity, and my Israeli identity card states my religion as Jewish. I could never have admitted on the Israeli side that I was now a Muslim named Yunus. To become a Muslim was like going over to the enemy, and I would surely have been considered a traitor.

I was Yonatan Shaked in the Jewish neighbourhood of East Talpiot and when I went to work, but when I on the Palestinian side I identified as a British Muslim, using my British Passport with the name John Robert Screeton. On the Palestinian side I had to hide my Jewish-Israeli identity of Yonatan Shaked because I would have been considered the enemy by the Palestinians.

I was living a double life. And if that was not enough, having built my Muslim identity on my British identity, I had resurrected John Robert Screeton.

That evening in East Talpiot, I decided to go to pray in the Arab neighbourhood of Beit Safafa, west of East Talpiot because I was well acquainted with Sheikh Abu Abdullah and members of the community there. After prayers I sat down with some of Sheikh Abu Abdullah's followers.

"Yunus, you must leave East Talpiot and get away from the Jews!" said one of the followers.

"And you must not waste your time with Bedouins!" said another.

"Sheikh Abu Abdullah will speak with Sheikh Raed Salah, the mayor of Umm al-fahm, and he will arrange for you to live and study Islam among good people, and you will be very happy there!" said another follower.

Umm al-fahm is an Israeli Arab city in the northern part of the country and, although I did not know much about it, it sounded a nice enough place to live and certainly a proposition worthwhile considering. I was tired of living a double identity and very much looked forward to settling down to a new life with new friends. It was clear to me that this was my fate.

Upon making inquiries about the city of Umm al-fahm I discovered, however, that the municipality was run by the Northern Islamic Movement, the hardline northern branch of the Islamic Movement in Israel. It turned out that the mayor, Sheikh Raed Salah, was suspected of raising funds in support of Hamas, a terrorist organisation.

I did not want to be an enemy of the State of Israel and therefore did not go to live in Umm al-fahm. I also cut off all ties with Sheikh Abu Abdullah and his followers; they held a deep hatred of the State of Israel and the Jews.

Chapter 20
The Aqabat-Jaber Refugee Camp

I drove down to Jericho by way of the old Roman Road route and stopped my car at the ridge overlooking Wadi Kelt. From there I scanned the hillsides in the hope of finding Khadra and her herd of goats, but as I listened to the deathly silence all around, a feeling of melancholy struck me. I stepped to the edge and looked down the deep rift to the *wadi* below, and I thought to myself, "It would be a relief to fall to my death."

A cold sweat came over me and I felt sick. I sat down on the firm ground and began to think about Sheikh Abu Abdullah and his followers — the people whom I had trusted — and I imagined what my life would have been if I had gone to live in Umm al-fahm. I shuddered at the thought.

There was no sign of Khadra, so I continued driving down towards Jericho and stopped at the spot where I had painted my watercolour when I first met Ahmad. I sat on the same rock and admired the familiar scene of flat and arable farm lands with distant hues of yellows and greens, but my mind wandered; I got lost in thought while gazing at the tiny, flat-roofed, mud houses in the foreground, and suddenly became aware of how lonely I was.

Jericho was like a shanty town, with a peculiar fascination about it. It was a sleepy town of intense heat where the men lounged about in idleness with not much motivation at all. I watched them strolling along the dirt paths, holding hands, or arm in arm.

Upon entering Jericho for the first time, I was struck by the strange assortment of wild-looking Bedouin men that came down from the encampments in the hills. They were a tough species, many of whom wore the traditional Bedouin attire of striped coats with knives in their leather belts, and they all had weathered skin, as tough as old leather. They had black, stained teeth and were unshaven. Indeed, they were a dirty bunch and reeked of perspiration from the oppressive heat that persistently drummed down upon them in the hills.

I walked towards the town centre, in the direction of the main street, past grubby men dressed in tight fitting, threadbare jeans with a strong smell of sweat. Occasionally I detected the heavy and foul smell of faeces from those who did not wash for prayers. The street gutters were black and oily, filled with the litter of rotting fruit, discarded cigarette packets, and crushed soft-drink cans. When passing the parking lot under the old sycamore trees, I choked on the black fumes that emitted from exhaust pipes of the shoddy looking cars. Taxi windows were adorned with red curtains and golden tassels, reminding me of Punch and Judy booths, and there were plastic flowers and ornaments hanging from rear-view mirrors. The drivers sat around scratching their crotches.

There were a few female Bedouins in traditional black robes, accompanied by males, but the shopping was done mainly by men alone. The purchases were made by the box-load and piled onto donkeys, or they hailed a Punch and Judy taxi cab to drive them back to their encampment in the hills.

Walking down the main street, I passed the bakery with pita breads laid out to cool on large floured wooden boards, and then I passed the local barber giving a client a soap-and-shave while the men queued patiently outside, awaiting their turn.

Slaughtered animals hung outside the butcher shop, and from within the screams and clucking of chickens could be heard from the stacks of wooden cages. I watched in awe as a customer chose a chicken and the butcher, seizing the screaming bird by the neck, took a knife and recited the words *Bismillah Allahu Akbar*, and cut its throat. I then watched as the headless chicken, still fluttering, was placed into a bucket of hot water and into a spinning contraption: within moments it was completely de-feathered. The stench of wet feathers and blood made me feel queasy and I hurried on.

Arabic music blared out from a cassette-player outside of a store plastered with posters of Umm Kulthum, which gave it a Holy Shrine appeal.

Men pushed and shoved along the sidewalk, their hands touching mine as they passed. Others, heavily laden with bags of groceries, walked in the road ignoring the honking cars.

Along the kerbside donkeys were tied up; their large black eyes lined with flies, skins twitching and tails swatting, and leaving heaps of steaming dung on the kerb.

I passed exotic scents that came from the spice store, aromatic freshly-ground coffee and cardamom from the coffee store, sugary fragrances from the sweet shop, and the clean smelling perfumes of laundry soaps that came from the grocery store. But then I passed a greasy, gas-operated rotisserie machine on the sidewalk, filled with skewered roasting chickens, the fat splashing and igniting, with huge clouds of vapour escaping the intense heat.

I continued on past a toy shop with battery operated cymbal-banging monkeys, a baby store with strollers, a men's clothing stores with British suit fabrics, and a women's store displaying chipped dummies dressed in Islamic tunics and headwear. Next to the Arab Bank, an electrical store sold twin-tub washing machines, and at the end of the street some market stalls were selling fresh fruit and vegetables. On display were clusters of ripe bananas, bunches of dates, honeydew melons with a sweet scent, and huge green water melons, some cut open revealing their juicy red centres. There were boxes of vegetables and fresh herbs, mallow leaves tied in bundles, and the yellow flowers of camomile: all produce of the fertile land, irrigated by natural springs, which made Jericho an oasis in the desert.

The adjacent streets were lined with old sycamore trees and a collection of shabby looking apartment buildings, and one small hotel, *the Jordan Hotel*. Walking further afield, however, I came upon a pleasant neighbourhood with beautiful summer homes belonging to wealthy Arabs. Here the streets were lined with red Bougainvillea and a variety of other flowering trees.

But as I was exploring this charming neighbourhood, I heard the call to prayer in the distance and hurried to the main mosque to make my ablutions.

The Bedouin tribe made inquiries for me about the possibility of renting an apartment in the centre of Jericho, but I wanted to get away from the noise and grime, and I wanted to be close to them. My wish was to wake up in the mornings to the scene of red mountains, to the smell of goats, and the sound of tin bells. I therefore decided to approach Hajji Abu Aref, one of the tribe's elders, who lived in the Aqabat-Jaber refugee camp.

As his title implied, he had made the *Hajj* pilgrimage to Mecca in Saudi Arabia. He was a good looking man with deep furrows that lined his dark skin, and his face resembled that of a mature male lion. Although getting on in age, he continued to take his herd of goats out to graze up in the mountains. Often, when I was hiking or seeking a quiet spot to meditate, I would come across him with his herd. He was always cordial towards me and for that reason I decided to approach him. And he happened to be Khadra's uncle.

Hajji Abu Aref lived with his aging wife in a home built of mud and straw bricks, within a compound surrounded by high walls built of the same mud and straw bricks. The entrance to the compound was through an old wooden gate that took one into a world of tiny, crookedly shaped huts, all weather beaten with traces of straw in the disintegrating mud bricks. It was desolate in appearance; the huts, the surrounding walls, and the ground were all the same desert sand colour.

The first hut was the *madafa*, where everyone gathered. There was a hut for Hajji Abu Aref and his wife, a hut for his daughters, and a hut for the goats. Each of the mud huts had one window with a view out of the compound towards the spectacular red mountains beyond. There was an outside kitchen covered by a roof of dried palm branches, with large cooking pots hanging over a pile of goat's dung. The dry pellets of dung were used as fuel in the underground oven, a hole in the ground in which the goat's dung was burned. When the goat's dung was smouldering hot, stones were laid upon it, and the bread dough was laid upon the stones, and then the oven was covered.

The toilet, where I made my ablutions, was very unpleasant. It was a small and oppressive cubicle built over a deep hole in the ground, made from broken pieces of plywood and other basic materials. Planks of wood were laid over the hole, leaving a small opening where one had to crouch and aim, evidently not with much success; there were layers upon layers of faeces that had dried around the opening. From the hole below, a heavy stench of urine and excrement rose up into the stifling hot cubicle.

There was no running water in the cubicle so I had to enter with a plastic container filled with water, to wash and remove all traces of urine and excrement from my body, as was required before prayers. After that I had to wash my hands, mouth, nostrils, face, arms, head, neck and ears and finally my feet — with the intention of being pure and clean which was a challenge while engulfed in the hot stench of fermenting excrement.

Hajji Abu Aref's wife was a plump old lady of ill health. She sat on the floor in the middle of the room, while smoking a cigarette.

The daughters did the household chores and washed the floor — around her. She had a full round face, with dark skin wrinkled like a baked apple, and only three teeth. Her hard-skinned feet were rough like the bark of an old tree trunk, and she had a serious fungal disease in her toe nails. I watched her anointing her feet and face with olive oil and expressed my concern to one of the daughters, but she just laughed at me.

"What do you expect?" she said. "She's already over one hundred years of age."

I had to agree. But it turned out that her daughter had a strange sense of humour and was joking. I was saddened to learn that the old lady was not yet seventy years old.

When I approached Hajji Abu Aref about the possibility of living in the same neighbourhood with them, he listened to my words in a civil manner and said that he would help me. He suggested that I build a house on a plot of land behind his house, close to the mountainside, and there, he said, I would have peace and quiet.

I wanted a house more than anything else, but I certainly could never have afforded to buy one on the Israeli side where the cost would have been hundreds of thousands of American dollars. The mere fact that I would be living in a refugee camp did not concern me, and therefore I immediately arranged for a building contractor to prepare the ground.

While the foundations for my new house were being prepared I slept in different locations, with various members of the tribe in Jericho, and occasionally in Wadi Kelt.

In Wadi Kelt, however, I discovered that a minor change had taken place. Whereas I had previously been attracted to the quiet and the way in which Suleiman's family sat in a circle and shared stories about their day, Suleiman had recently purchased a portable, twelve inch black-and-white television set which operated on a car battery. *Now* they sat in front of the television set, with the volume turned up to its highest setting, and they were completely spellbound by it.

It had become unbearable on Suleiman's side of the *wadi*, and therefore I went to sleep on the other side of the *wadi* in the flourmill.

One morning, Atta's younger brother showed me how he slaughters a goat in the Islamic way. He took the goat, said the words *Bismillah Allahu Akba,* and hacked away at its throat with a blunt knife. The poor creature choked on its own blood and gasped for breath through its perforated windpipe; the sight was so appalling that my stomach turned and I almost threw up.

That evening I was invited by Suleiman and his family to eat on their side of the *wadi*. I was served *mansaf,* a traditional dish that is usually served on special occasions consisting of goat's meat cooked in a strong flavoured yogurt, served on bread and rice. We all sat on the floor around the large platter, but first we recited the words *Bismillah ir-Rahman ir-Rahim,* and then we began eating.

Suddenly Jasser burst out laughing.

"What happened to you, Jasser?" I asked, completely taken aback.

"It's your friend!" he replied, giggling.

"*What's* my friend? I asked, his words making no sense.

"You're eating *Samour!*"

I realised that we were eating my favourite goat, the goat that had followed me and nibbled at my fingers, and I was horrified. I jumped up with the intention of leaving, but Jasser was rolling on the floor laughing at me. None of them could understand my reaction.

Around this time news reached me of yet another double killing in Wadi Kelt. Two women hikers, lovers of nature, were stabbed to death and had their throats cut. Their bodies were found thrown down into the *wadi*.

I continued visiting Hajji Abu Aref in Jericho to see how my house was progressing, and occasionally I went into town to pray at the mosque.

After prayers one day, someone greeted me: "*Assalamu Alaikum,* Yunus!"

It was Ahmad dressed in a black cloak with a gold trim, and I had not recognised him at all.

"*Wa Alaikum Assalamu, Mukhtar* Ahmad," I replied, surprised to see him dressed so dignified.

Apparently Ahmad had been to a meeting with Yasser Arafat at the Palestinian National Authority.

"Yunus, please meet me at my home afterwards. I would like to talk to you."

I walked to Ahmad's house and waited outside the *madafa*. The weather was pleasant, and I sat in the warm sun with my eyes closed enjoying the peace and quiet, but after a while I sensed Ahmad's presence.

"Yunus," he said, "I'm going to bring us something to eat."

I closed my eyes again, enjoying the warm sun.

Ahmad returned with a large tray, full of delicious food, and while we were eating he spoke to me about *Hadith* – the traditions and activities of the Prophet Muhammad. I always found his stories stimulating.

We finished eating and went for a walk to the mouth of the *wadi*. Along the way Ahmad showed me the various herbs and edible plants that grow naturally in the wild, and he told me stories from the *Hadith* about those herbs and plants.

Finally we came to the place where we had first met; the very rock where I painted my first watercolour of Jericho, and the place where my romance with the Bedouins started many years before.

Ahmad then began telling me that according to Bedouin tradition people marry within the tribe. He said that a man is permitted to bring a girl from the outside; however, a girl from the tribe would *never* be allowed to marry a man from outside of the tribe.

I then understood the purpose of our rendezvous and challenged him.

"Ahmad, you are constantly reminding me that I'm your brother. Therefore, why can't I marry a Bedouin girl from your tribe?"

"Yunus, *ya haram*, you must not talk to Khadra ever again!"

"This is not the way of Islam!" I argued.

"Yunus, *this* is the way of the Bedouins!" he answered. "And Yunus, you must stop building your house – for your own sake!" I looked at him in bewilderment. "After you complete it, Abu Aref's sons will claim it! Stop it now, *I insist!*"

Ahmad refused to discuss the matter any further and walked away, leaving me alone on the rock. The nerves in my face twitched, and I could not move. I was in a state of shock. After some time, however, and with a heavy heart, I went to my car and drove home to my apartment in Jerusalem.

Along the way I began singing! I suddenly felt that I had been relieved of a great burden; the burden of having to marry Khadra, the burden of the house in Jericho, and the burden of being a Muslim.

I continued singing all the way home, but by the time I arrived the conflict within me had completely drained me. I collapsed onto my bed and fell into a deep sleep.

When I awoke I got the scare of my life: only then did I realise that I had been living a lie all along.

I felt ill and developed a severe migraine, and I could not face life anymore. I remained at home on sick leave for three days and did not pray or do anything. I had come to a dead-end.

Initially, I saw myself as a Jew, living in Jerusalem with a loving wife and little boys with side-curls, wearing yarmulkes and the ritual fringes, but my dream was shattered. Then I saw myself as a Muslim, married to a Bedouin girl with Bedouin children, a herd of goats and a house in Jericho but once again my dream had been shattered.

Above all, however, I had failed to overcome my homosexuality. I realised that I would never have a family of my own and asked

God, "Why did You make me a homosexual if I don't want to be a homosexual?"

The notion of not having children upset me greatly, and I began to wonder what meaning there would be to life without continuation. I decided that I would help others to have children and therefore, twice a week for a whole year I went to the hospital sperm bank to masturbate into a cup so that women could be impregnated by artificial insemination. I donated over one hundred portions of sperm so that *they* could have the children I could not have.

Chapter 21
Hebron

The Bedouins were hospitable and very warm towards me; I never experienced such love in my entire life as I did with the Bedouins, which is perhaps why after my small crisis that I caught up with my lost prayers and salvaged my Muslim identity. On one hand I had come to a dead-end, but on the other hand I wanted to belong, and so I kept on going in the same direction.

However, Jericho was not an option anymore so now I looked towards Hebron.

Ahmad had an older brother who lived near Hebron and I began to spend my time with him. Eid was a religious man who lived with his two wives and children in a house that he had built in a quiet corner, bordering on a forest. To get to his house I took the Hebron Road, and just before the city of Hebron I turned off down a narrow lane. I had the forest on my left side, and on my right side were endless cherry orchards with a view of the Judean Mountains. I parked my car next to the broken-down garden wall and walked up a gravel path between the vineyards. The house, set further back in the forest, was hidden by a large fig tree. There were steps that led up to a large veranda, enclosed by ornate wrought iron windows, and which acted as the *madafa*. Mattresses and cushions were arranged neatly all around the room, ready for guests.

Eid introduced me to his large family, and then took me to his private room where he studied the Qur'an. In it was an old wooden desk piled high with dog-eared exercise books and the Holy Qur'an. There was also a three piece living room suite covered in nylon stretch-covers with frilly edging, and in the centre of the room a metal coffee table with an acrylic glass surface. On the coffee table were a couple of pastel coloured tin vases filled with faded plastic flowers. The musty room was his pride and joy.

Eid was employed by the Israeli Nature and Parks Authority at the Dead Sea, and came home to his two wives only on the weekends. When at home he wore his green uniform with pride, even when off-duty. He was of stocky build with a rugged look; his dark skin was heavily lined and he looked much older than his age. And yet, his eyes were a clear green and his hair and moustache were jet black.

Except for my initial introduction I rarely saw the wives and daughters; they were kept in a separate part of the house where no one else entered. Whenever I stayed with Eid he would play host, with his sons acting as liaison between him and his wives in the other part of the house. The sons served the meals and also cleaned up afterwards. They were fine boys with a deep respect for their father.

Mustafa, who was the eldest son, would sleep with me in the musty room when I stayed over for the night. He was very much like his father: a pedantic and religious person who made a point of praying on time, and frequently quoted from the Holy Qur'an and from the *Hadith*. He was a policeman in the Palestinian Authority Police Force and was always well groomed. He had stunning jade-green eyes, an olive complexion, light brown hair, and he looked strikingly handsome in his dark blue police uniform.

In our conversations at night I found that we had something in common. Like me, Mustafa loved nature and sought inner peace. Beneath the military façade, I discovered that he was a tender young man and we became good friends. Consequently, we went on vacation together across the border to Jordan, and there we hired a car to see the sights and to travel the length of the country.

We started our vacation in the southern Red Sea resort of Aqaba and gradually made our way north by way of Wadi Rum, staying in Wadi Musa from where we visited the ancient city of Petra. We continued our journey to Al Karak, on the Jordanian side of the Dead Sea, spending the day at the spa, and then we stopped for a few days in Amman. From there we travelled to Jerash, Ajlun and finally to Umm Qais in the north where I had a peculiar sensation; I was admiring the view there, but then I realised that the magnificent scenery was over the border in Israel.

In the morning Eid knocked on the door to wake us for the Dawn Prayer and left a jug of warm water for me to make my ablutions, but for this I had to go outside into the dark forest before the crack of dawn. I crept upon a soft carpet of pine-needles, with the sharp snap of twigs echoing through the silent forest, and found a tree to hide behind. It was surreal being alone in the forest while making my ablutions and listening to the chirping of the birds as they awoke, with the dark trees silhouetted against an early morning sky. I hurried back to the veranda, stepping bare-foot upon the cold floor tiles, and took my place on the prayer mat next to the brothers, with Eid leading the prayers as Imam.

After prayers I had breakfast with Eid in his room, graciously served by his sons. They smiled and listened politely to their father's many requests: to bring more bread, to put mint in the tea, to bring *dibs* (a type of syrup made from grapes) and they carried out their duties honourably. When we were finally left alone, I listened attentively to Eid's stories while observing his sensual lips, the lines in his dark skin, his strong white teeth and his black hair. I was full of admiration for the way in which he raised his sons.

After we had finished breakfast Mustafa took me to the vineyards to work with him. He taught me how to prune the vines, and to do shoot thinning, and leaf removal. He told me that the leaves were saved for his two mothers to stuff with meat and rice. Eid came to visit us with a tray of tea and a plate of dates, and after he had inspected our work — and expressed his satisfaction — we sat down on the hard, dry soil, under the shade of the vines, and we drank our tea. In conversation, Eid suggested that we drive to Hebron to pray in the Ibrahimi Mosque, which seemed like a good idea, And so we made our ablutions, applied some musk perfume, and set out on our journey.

Along the way we passed the glassblowing factories with stunning displays of glass floats and vases in vivid blues and greens, and then we entered the Old City of Hebron. I parked my car, but as we approached the great stairway that leads up to the Ibrahimi Mosque, I had a strange sensation. It suddenly dawned on me that the Ibrahimi Mosque was in fact the Cave of the Patriarchs!

According to Jewish tradition the Cave of the Patriarchs is where Abraham and Sara, Isaac and Rebecca, and Jacob and Leah were buried in a cave purchased by Abraham to become the family tomb, in a contract of sale recorded in the Book of Genesis.

And yet we were entering a mosque.

After we finished praying in the mosque, Eid took me to see a large and impressive tomb covered in luxurious green velvet with gold Islamic calligraphy embroidered on it. It was in an attractive vaulted room, painted in shades of blue and pink, but I noticed a family of ultra-Orthodox Jews peering in through a small barred window, from a corridor on the other side. This was a horrible sight for me to see, and it shocked me that Jews were restricted from entering.

I was so troubled by our visit to the mosque that I asked Eid this question: "Why is it Abraham, Isaac and Jacob are considered to be Muslim prophets, when in fact they are the Patriarchs and ancestors of Judaism from many hundreds of years before the existence of Islam?"

My question was seen by Eid as a breach of faith.

"Yunus, all the prophets were Muslims!" he said sternly.

I knew that this was what Muslims believed, and yet I did not understand it. And besides, part of me was rebelling after seeing the tomb covered in Islamic calligraphy while ultra-Orthodox Jews were peering in through bars from the other side. It did not seem right.

Then Eid quoted from the *Hadith*:

Those who were best in the pre-Islamic period are the best in Islam...

I was stunned.

I was well aware that the Muslims had taken over Jewish religious sites in the land of Israel, as they had done on the Temple Mount, the holiest site for the Jews, where they had built the Dome of the Rock shrine and the Al-Aqsa Mosque. But on this day at the Cave of the Patriarchs in Hebron, it occurred to me that Islam had also taken over the Jewish Prophets interred in the ground.

Later that evening I drove home to my apartment in East Talpiot, passing Rachel's Tomb in Bethlehem, the burial place of the Matriarch Rachel, but now a mosque.

When at home in my apartment, I began to understand the complexity of Islam. "Islam" means *submission to the will of God.* The meaning of "Muslim" is *one who submits to God*, and therefore the past prophets were Muslims *because* they were Jews! It suddenly seemed outrageously absurd that the Jewish descendants of Abraham mentioned in the Bible *are the best in Islam*!

I was angry that Islam had kidnapped the dead Jewish Prophets, taking them against their will, and had made them into

Muslims. But by doing so, the Muslims had changed the past and consequently *believe* that all the Jewish holy sites belong to them!

That night, chaos filled my head: "What have I done?" I cried.

I tossed and turned in my bed as the thoughts tore at me from my inside.

Chapter 22
The Valley of Elah

I did physical exercises, and I frequently ran around the perimeter of East Talpiot to maintain my fitness and overall good health. Occasionally I ran through Jabel Mukaber, the neighbouring Arab village, and over the years I made friends there. Even the children were accustomed to seeing me and would chant, *"Yehudi! Yehudi!"* as I ran by. For them I was still a Jew from the other side.

On this particular day, as I ran, I began to feel as heavy as lead; as if the force of gravitation had accelerated. It pulled me down to the ground. "It's the end of the world," I thought to myself as I lay glued to the tarmac, too heavy for my legs to carry me. It was like a bad dream, I wanted to run but I could not move.

I managed to drag myself home and had a hot shower and something to eat. When I was feeling better I masturbated, but a sharp pain shot through my head and I could not reach ejaculation. The next day the pain had subsided — although it did not leave me entirely — and I masturbated again. This time, however, an excruciating pain shot to my head and I fell onto the floor. The next thing I remember was me being on the express train to hell; the glaring lights zoomed past me as I fell down into the afterlife.

Actually I was being wheeled down a never ending corridor on a hospital stretcher with a blond, female doctor firing questions at me:

"Do you have AIDS?" she shouted.

I was unable to answer or even think.

"Do you have AIDS? Do you have AIDS?" she kept repeating.

I made a feeble attempt to talk: "No... I... do... not... have... *AIDS*!" My head throbbed with each syllable that I spoke.

"How do you know? Have you been tested? What's your name?"

I could not understand *why* she was asking me if I had AIDS.

"Doctor, I don't have AIDS because I don't have sex!"

But the look on her face told me that she did not believe me.

"I didn't have sex for over twenty years, so how can I?" I declared.

"Are you taking drugs?" she asked.

"No! No sex, no alcohol, no cigarettes and no drugs!"

After blood tests and a lumbar puncture I was diagnosed with meningitis. I remained in hospital for a number of weeks, but after I was discharged I remained under observation in the neurology outpatient clinic. The feeling of confusion that comes with meningitis never left me. I was constantly tired and was also diagnosed with Chronic Fatigue Syndrome, but due to my worsened mental state I was referred to the psychiatric outpatient clinic as well.

My psychiatrist was a young, modern-Orthodox Jew doing his internship in the hospital. He had black wavy hair, a Roman nose and dark eyes, and he was strikingly handsome. He encouraged me to make a change in my life and suggested that I go to live in a new environment. At the time I was in a serious emotional state and desperately wanted to get better, and the proposition of a new life in a new environment appealed to me a lot. My psychiatrist was my saviour and I believed that it was the right thing to do. I therefore gave up my government-controlled apartment that I was renting in East Talpiot, and I rented a house in the private sector on Moshav Givat Yeshayahu, an agricultural village, in the Valley of Elah.

The house was pleasant enough, with a large veranda shaded by a sycamore tree where I could relax to the sounds of nature; the birds in the trees, the distant bleating of sheep, and the quiet. I made the interior of the house presentable with silk curtains from India, and I covered my divan with an emerald green, cotton cover and added some throw-pillows in vibrant reds. Above the divan I hung a large watercolour of Jerusalem — which I had painted — flanked by a pair of wall-lights from the flea market in Jaffa. On two side tables I placed copper lamps with lamp-shades which I covered in black Bedouin veils decorated in pink sequins and golden coins. Over the broken floor tiles I placed dark red, hand-woven rugs which I had bargained for in the Old City of Jerusalem. I filled the book shelves with books and knickknacks, and in the centre of the room I hung an Italian brass chandelier.

After designing the interior of my new home, I began to spend time outside in the garden. Gardening had been a childhood love of mine, and now I had the opportunity to take care of my own garden which brought back some good memories of England. I planted cyclamens under the sycamore tree, and daffodils and tulips all around the borders, and my garden bloomed. My new life and surroundings gave me a feeling of wellbeing, and I managed to build up a fine tan while working outside in just a pair of shorts.

I took bicycle rides down country lanes, and along the way I discovered extensive vineyards, silver-grey olive plantations, and peach orchards tinted with pink blossom. I continued riding on, past oaks and terebinth trees, and came to a hill covered with a spectacular array of blue lupins. I sat down on the dry, warm earth to admire the Valley of Elah, where the Israelites had once encamped, and I imagined David hurling a stone from his sling and killing the giant warrior Goliath.

I went for walks around the *moshav*, admiring the community and their modest homes with well-kept gardens, and I fantasised owning a house on the *moshav*. I felt very happy in my new environment, with the magnificent views over the Valley of Elah. It was the Israel I loved; of green hills, *moshavim* and *kibbutzim* with the smell of cowsheds and chicken coops.

My psychiatrist, however, insisted that I must go to work, and therefore I took employment at Ben Gurion International Airport. The experience was devastating. I was pushed back into a world that I did not belong in: the crowds, the noise, and the constant airport announcements overwhelmed me. My head throbbed, the nerves in my face began to twitch, and I could not concentrate when people spoke to me. I went to the public bathroom, where the bright lights made me feel nauseous, and splashed my face with cold water. When I looked up in the mirror I saw a haggard old man looking back at me. That evening I resigned from the job.

My savings began to dwindle and I foresaw that if I did not find a solution, I would not be able to continue paying rent and would soon be homeless. When I informed my landlady that I would be leaving, she told me I could stay without paying rent. She was a warm and very kind lady, and I know that she was concerned about my welfare, but I could not impose myself upon her. In any case, I had another plan.

I drove down to Wadi Kelt to discuss my plan with Suleiman.

"Yunus! *Ahlan wa Sahlan*!" Suleiman cried. "Where have you been all this time?"

I was a bit slow on the uptake after my illness, and when I heard the name Yunus, the memory of my Muslim identity hit me and I stood there momentarily stunned.

I began telling Suleiman that I had been ill for the past year, but I broke down crying. He was troubled by what he saw and called Fatimah to come out, explaining to her in Arabic what had happened to me.

"*Salamtak* Yunus," said Fatimah, with a concerned look. She shook hands with me for the first time.

I tried to compose myself but was badly shaken up, and I was confused being in Wadi Kelt once again; but I desperately needed Suleiman's help. I was a broken person with nowhere to live.

Fatimah hurried off to make tea, and I sat down with Suleiman to ask if I could put up a tent in the *wadi*, stressing that I was ill and needed to be alone. Suleiman listened attentively, but he informed me that I would need permission from the authorities to live in the *wadi*. He promised to discuss the matter with Eid, adding that I was welcome to stay with him until a solution was worked out. His words were a great comfort to me.

As we drank our tea Atta walked over from the flourmill, and upon hearing about my illness he kissed me and gave me a hug.

"Yunus, my brother," said Atta. "You will live with us in the flourmill, in the room next to the goats. *Ahlan wa Sahlan!*"

I was touched by their kindness, but as I was about to take my leave, Atta said: "Yunus, come and pray with me!"

For a moment I was speechless. Ever since my illness I had blocked out Yunus and my Muslim identity, but now I did not know what to say.

"I have forgotten how to pray," I said, timidly.

"*Insha'Allah* you will learn again," he replied.

"*Insha'Allah!*" I said, but his words rang in my head like an alarm.

The next time that I went to my psychiatrist I announced my plan to him. He sat quite still, staring at me, and did not say a word. The silence seemed to last forever, but at last he spoke.

"Yonatan, you have to rent an apartment," he said in his gentle manner.

"And *who* will pay for it – *you?*" I responded violently.

"Go to work," he answered, casually.

I shuddered at the proposition. "I *cannot* work! I *hate* this world; I *hate* people; I *hate* my life, and it's because of you that I'm in this predicament!"

"Why?" he asked, calmly.

"Because you should never have encouraged me to leave my government-controlled apartment in Jerusalem; I could have continued living there rent-free and not be homeless, *that's why!*"

We sat there in silence but eventually I pulled my heavy body out of the chair and left without a word.

I headed for the psychiatric clinic's exit door, fearing he would come after me, and he surely did; I heard him calling me, his voice echoed down the corridor, *"Yonatan! Yonatan!"* but I imagined him locking me up and made a quick run for it.

My life on Moshav Givat Yeshayahu in the Valley of Elah had been a nice fantasy. Within one week I dismantled the contents of the house, put everything into storage, and I sold my car. With just a rucksack on my back, I headed for Wadi Kelt.

Chapter 23
The Garden of Eden

The entrance to my room in the flourmill had a derelict door of rotting wood that was falling off its hinges; I needed all my strength just to open it. Inside, the room had a great vaulted ceiling and the bare brick walls were almost one metre thick. There were no windows except for one narrow vertical opening in the thick wall. It was dark and cold inside.

Scattered over the concrete floor I found a couple of cotton mattresses and some blankets which I took outside for a good shaking. I arranged them neatly on the cold floor, and using my rucksack as a pillow, I lay down and whispered to the walls: "Home sweet home." I was grateful to have a place to live.

At night the room was pitch-dark. It seemed as if I was sleeping in a tomb; there was not a sound inside. I slept a deep sleep but in the morning was awoken by Atta banging on the door for me to come and eat breakfast. Upon opening the door, I was blinded by the painfully bright sunlight – and stunned by the strong tang of goat's urine.

Atta had just finished the milking but was doing a survey of the goats. He giggled when he saw me in my soiled *Gallabiyah* with a

Keffiyeh tied crudely around my head. When on my way to the aqueduct to wash my face, the aroma of warm milk still lingered in the air

Atta had become more religious and now commanded both his wives to wear burqas, to conceal their faces and bodies while in public. Unlike in the past, I had to eat my breakfast alone with Atta. Hanya, his vivacious first wife, was forbidden to talk with me.

Breakfast consisted of a potently flavoured curd cheese, olive oil and freshly baked bread. It was expected of me to eat with Atta in the evenings too, but occasionally Suleiman invited me to eat with him on the other side of the *wadi*. This caused Atta to give me a look of disapproval.

"Yunus, you live here, so you must eat *with me!*" he said with a twinkle in his eyes.

After Atta left with his herd of goats each morning, I wandered upstream in the direction of the waterfall. I took the dirt path, adjacent to the aqueduct, and sensed the desert heat rising up with the odours of the *wadi*; warm urine with goat droppings, and the sweet and grassy fragrance of reeds that grew by the aqueduct. I stopped to observe the schools of tiny fish that glistened as they swam upstream against the current, and I detected a fishy smell that came from the water as it raced down to Jericho.

At the waterfall I bathed in the pool to the meditative sound of plunging waters. Afterwards I lay down on the warm rock while listening to the fascinating calmness that fell upon the *wadi* in the heat of the day. I felt intoxicated, immersed in my new surroundings, with the distant croaking of frogs and sounds of nature echoing down the *wadi*. Occasionally, on my wanderings, I stopped to rest under the shade of a tree to listen to the calming sounds. In the afternoons, Hanya sent me a pot of tea and something to eat with one of her children.

And so the weeks passed until Suleiman informed me that a solution had been reached regarding a permanent place for me to live in the *wadi*.

It had been decided that I would stay in the *bustan*, a fenced-in garden close to the flourmill, where I would be able to build a tent. A representative from the Israeli Nature and Parks Authority came to authorize it, and the next day Eid came down to Wadi Kelt to take me into the *bustan*.

The *bustan* had not been attended to for many years and was an overgrown mass of thistles and prickles. We entered through an old rusty gate that was tied to a post with a hefty chain, and then we waded through the dry thistles, some of which were over three metres tall, to the other side of the bustan. There we came to a palm tree, where I would build my tent, and we cleared some of the undergrowth and sat down gazing directly into a forest of weeds.

"Yunus, this used to be my father's *bustan*," said Eid, reminiscing of old times, "but it's neglected because Suleiman and Atta do nothing! I want you to take care of it."

"I'd be more than happy to do that," I answered.

Eid took some almonds out of his bag, and we shared them in contented silence.

The following day, after breakfast, I started the job of clearing the *bustan* of the thistles and prickles. Towards evening time, when Atta came down the mountainside with his herd, he jumped off his donkey and came to visit me while I was still hard at work.

"Yunus, why don't you stay in the flourmill with me?" he asked with a baffled look.

It was true that I was content in the flourmill, but I wanted to be completely alone and independent. And besides, I knew that I could make the *bustan* into a paradise.

I began building the tent by first putting up a Sukkah frame, used by religious Jews for the festival of *Sukkot*. Suleiman brought me a pile of hessian sacks from Jericho, and I began sewing them together to make the tent that would cover the Sukkah frame. When Atta saw me sewing, he came and sewed with me, but then he took a bundle of the sacks and gave them to his wives to sew – and we all sewed for three days.

When all of us had finished, I fitted the sweet smelling hessian sacks over my Sukkah frame and named it the *Sukkah-Tent*. I covered the ground with straw matting and placed upon it two cotton mattresses with cushions in typical Bedouin style. Next to my Sukkah-Tent I built a kitchen and a shower room made from pieces of old plywood, and I used a hose to syphon water from the aqueduct.

I then set out to work on the *bustan*. I used a pick axe to hoe the land and built a network of canals and an irrigation system, directing the syphoned water to the loquat trees, to the date palms, and to a vegetable patch where I sowed seeds of herbs, tomatoes, marrows and other vegetables in the freshly turned earth. The *bustan* was transformed into a small paradise.

At this stage I purchased a mobile-phone and the first call that I made was to my psychiatrist. It had been a long while since we had spoken, but he agreed that I should resume psychotherapy and made me an appointment to come to see him.

I shaved and showered, creamed my hair, polished my shoes, and after applying a little musk oil I climbed to the top of the *wadi* and hailed a bus to Jerusalem. The contrast, however, between living down in the *wadi* and the real world outside was overwhelming. Suddenly there were people everywhere, and all I wanted to do was run back to my paradise in Wadi Kelt. The moment I reached the hospital I purchased an espresso coffee and found refuge in a quiet corner. I sat down and observed a bustling world that I did not belong to with faces everywhere, and each face was labeled Muslim, Jew, or Christian.

My psychiatrist gave me an ultimatum.

"Yonatan, you have to rent an apartment. No apartment: no therapy," he said.

"Oh no, Doctor, please don't do this to me; I am happy in Wadi Kelt!" I pleaded.

"Why do you want to live with dirty Bedouins in unhygienic conditions?" he asked.

"Do *I* look dirty to you?" I asked, knowing that I looked immaculate.

"No apartment: no therapy," he repeated.

Nothing was more important to me than psychotherapy. I needed to know that there was hope and that I could deal with my issues, but this new strategy terrified me. I argued with him, but he insisted that I have to go to work and rent an apartment. He repeated the mantra, "no apartment: no therapy," and refused to treat me.

I was devastated. I wandered the streets of Jerusalem, ending up in the emergency room of the Talbieh Psychiatric Hospital where I stayed overnight. When I went back to Wadi Kelt I fell into a dark place, and all the stamina with which I had built my Sukkah-Tent, completely drained from me. The feeling of wellbeing turned into depression, and I was overcome with fears. I lay on my mattress, too tired to get up, and at night I heard strange sounds: I lived in fear of being slaughtered in my bed. I confided in Suleiman about my fears and he arranged for his son, Taisir, to sleep with me in the Sukkah-Tent every night.

Atta also came regularly to visit me in my Sukkah-Tent. He was fascinated how I prepared my vegetables with garlic, and how I stir-fried everything in olive oil with herbs and dried Persian lemons. He was so intrigued by the way that I cooked my food that he came every day and ate with me. We scooped up my concoction with pita bread, straight out of the frying-pan.

"Atta, should you not be eating with your two wives?" I asked one evening.

"I prefer it here!" he answered.

After eating, he would recline on the mattress and smoke his *nargileh* water pipe, and I would fall asleep to the meditative sound of bubbling water. I awoke only when I heard Taisir enter and Atta leaving, but I slept soundly every night knowing that Taisir was there.

As time passed I became a permanent fixture in the *bustan*. I was like a Sheikh to whom the boys in the *wadi* came to confide in; they would ask me for advice, and they told me their deepest secrets.

Throughout the *bustan*, the air was filled with the sweet perfume of loquat trees; the tiny white flowers glimmered like pearls upon the dark, leathery green leaves, and from the tiny white flowers grew clusters of velvety yellow fruit, large and succulent. The *bustan* bloomed and the news spread quickly; Bedouins came from afar, as if on a pilgrimage, and named the *bustan* the Garden of Eden. The women cried with joy upon seeing the kitchen and shower, and the men were astonished to see a vegetable patch filled with vegetables. The boys in the *wadi* climbed the loquat trees and picked the fruit.

Then Eid came and surveyed the grounds. He sat with me in my Sukkah-Tent and could not hide his joy, but he was angry that people were stealing his fruit.

"Yunus, you must not let anyone enter the gate! This is *my* land and *my* trees. I forbid it!" he said.

A few days later Jasser came with a group of boys and entered the *bustan*. They climbed the trees and gathered the fruit in bundles. I came out of the Sukkah-Tent and told Jasser that Eid forbids anyone from entering his *bustan*.

"It's not Eid's *bustan*!" Jasser yelled; "it's my father's *bustan*!"

Taking a rock in his right hand, he held it up high, and roared: "And *who* are *you* to tell me this?"

Jasser hurled the rock at me. It almost hit me in the face, but if it had I surely could have been killed. But then he took another rock, and another, and another, and aimed them at me. The other boys begged him to stop but he was out of control, like a madman. He picked up a heavy, thorny palm branch and came running at me, and beat me with it repeatedly until I fell to the ground bleeding.

And then they all ran away.

I could not get up at first; the pain shot down my back, but then I saw that I was bleeding badly. I called out for help, but there was a scary silence in the *wadi* and no one came. At that moment I realised that I could be in danger and thought to myself, "They will come back and finish me off."

I had to run to safety.

Luckily it was a Saturday, the Jewish Sabbath, and I remembered that since the murders in Wadi Kelt the Israel Defence Forces came on the Sabbath to guard Israeli tourists at the waterfall. I prayed with all my might that they would be there.

I limped in the direction of the waterfall but my back was hurting and my chest was tight from anxiety. All along the way I feared that Jasser would come after me. As I hobbled along the dirt path, adjacent to the aqueduct, I was horrified when I saw Taisir coming down the mountainside towards me; terror gripped me as I imagined that they were surrounding me, and I was sure that they were going to kill me.

I noticed, however, that Taisir was smiling innocently, and I understood that he was unaware of what had transpired in the *bustan*. I faked cheerfulness and hurried on towards the waterfall with my heart thumping against my chest. Then I heard the faint sound of army Walkie-Talkies, and as I approached the soldiers I collapsed.

The soldiers began to call in reinforcements and I heard them referring to it as a terrorist attack. I told them, however, that it was not a terrorist attack and that the Bedouins were my friends, but because I had been attacked and was wounded with blood, they considered me to be in danger and called in extra ground troops.

In the meantime a medic cleaned and dressed my wounds, on the same rock that I had lain upon on so many occasions. I lay there listening to the familiar sound of plunging waters, but then the commander informed me that they were taking me out to safety. My thoughts shot back to my Sukkah-Tent in the *bustan*, and I asked him if I could take some personal belongings. The commander immediately arranged for the troops to surround the *bustan*, and he accompanied me into the Sukkah-Tent and sat down in the easy chair while I packed my rucksack and dressed into clean clothes. He was impressed by my Sukkah-Tent.

"This is the kind of place I would like to bring my girl-friend," he said.

When I was ready, he put my rucksack on his shoulder and led me to an army truck that awaited me on the other side of the *wadi*.

Chapter 24
Alone

After a medical examination I walked out of the Emergency Room and stood gazing into a world that I did not know; I looked at the real world and a shudder went through me like an electric shock. My world, the world of Wadi Kelt and the *bustan*, had suddenly been taken from me.

"Why did he do it?" I lamented.

I had nowhere to go, so I telephoned Joel who lived close by, and he came quickly. But when he arrived with that knowing look on his face, and said to me: "I *told* you so!" I decided there and then *not* to go with him and called another friend. I was a broken person; the cuts and bruises would heal but I was traumatized and could not understand Jasser's behaviour. At that moment I felt that I would break down crying and could not endure Joel's insensitivity. I went to my other friend who lived on a religious settlement in Gush Etzion, south of Bethlehem. They were hospitable people but I carried the burden of my trauma, and I needed to find another solution. I could not be with people the way that I was feeling; I needed to be alone, and I wanted to be somewhere neutral, and not in a religious environment.

My psychiatrist was of no help, and out of desperation I approached the local rabbi who offered me a room in the *Yeshiva* — but on the condition that I wear a yarmulke. I was not prepared to do that, and therefore I called Joel on my mobile phone and told him about a new plan.

Joel worked in a small factory that produced ritual fringes and blue dye – for it is written:

Speak unto the Children of Israel, and bid them that they make them throughout their generations fringes in the corner of their garments, and that they put with the fringe of each corner a thread of blue.

The factory was located next to an abandoned plant nursery near Kfar Adumim, just off the highway that leads to Jericho. Here I planned to rebuild my Sukkah-Tent, but first I needed to salvage it from Wadi Kelt.

Joel was brave enough to drive me down to the bottom of Wadi Kelt, which was deserted when we arrived. We cautiously made our way over the dry river bed to the other side, but my heart pounded as the memory of the attack came pouring back. It had been almost three months since the attack, but as we approached the *bustan* gate I was deeply distressed by what I saw. It was a mass of thistles and prickles once again, my vegetable garden was parched dry and everything had shriveled up and died. Worst of all, the contents of my Sukkah-Tent had been ransacked and it was a horrible sight to see.

We quickly disassembled the Sukkah-Tent, but as we were working I saw someone approaching and stepped back in fear. It was Atta, but he had come in peace and expressed his regret over what had happened. As I looked at him in his dirty *Gallabiyah* I wanted to hug and kiss him but instead I shook hands – and so did Joel, somewhat reluctantly – and then we left with what remained of my Sukkah-Tent.

I reassembled my Sukkah-Tent in a quiet corner, on the grounds of the abandoned nursery, in a place where I could be completely alone. I wanted to keep a neutral identity and did not want to identify as a Jew or as a Muslim.

Ironically I was less than five kilometres away from the Bedouins in Wadi Kelt, situated high above the *wadi*, and with a splendid view over the Judaean Desert. I spent much of my day wandering the hills in search of dry wood to keep a fire burning so that I could make Bedouin tea and cook my meals. Work in Joel's factory was done by hand so it was quiet in my Sukkah-Tent. In the evenings, when they closed up the factory and had gone home, there was not a sound to be heard and I lived a peaceful existence — completely alone.

Each evening I sat in my easy chair watching the sun set, while listening to the silence. As night time fell I was surrounded by a mysterious blackness, a void all around, and watched the flames in the fire burn down; just the smouldering embers remained in the dark. I could feel myself becoming heavy and numb from sitting so long, and I had to pull my heavy body out of the chair to prepare the evening meal.

Every night I prepared the same meal in the glow of the fire. I cut up vegetables, garlic and onions, stirred in tomatoes, zucchinis and sweet red peppers, while kneeling in front of the hot, red fire. I ate my meal from the frying pan with pita bread, and then I prepared Bedouin tea. I drank my tea in the easy chair while staring into the smouldering fire, slowly becoming hypnotized by it as it burned down to a cinder.

Gradually I adjusted to my new surroundings and began to wander further afield. I took walks to the stark hill tops, enjoying the fresh mountain air, and occasionally I saw gazelles leaping across the peaks. I ventured on, down the other side of the mountainous terrain, exploring the caves and hideouts along the way. I descended the mountainside until I reached to the bottom of the *wadi*. At the bottom I discovered the Ein Fawwar spring, one of the springs along the Wadi Kelt riverbed, and I stopped to rest by the pool. I watched Arab and Jewish children playing side by side in the water but my eyes were drawn up, towards the caves hewn into the side of the canyon, and I contemplated the possibility of living in one of the caves.

After a while I found myself thinking more and more about my Bedouin family; they were so close and yet so far away. My life in the *wadi* had ended abruptly, but my Bedouin family and lifestyle still remained very much a part of me. I missed them a lot, and I could not bear the pain and loss anymore, for in my heart I still loved them. After some hesitation, I telephoned Eid on my mobile-phone.

"Eid, it's Yunus speaking," I said.

I was very excited to talk to him again.

"Yunus – listen to me! You made a serious mistake by going to the Israeli Army – *to the enemy!*" he shouted.

"But, Eid, I was in danger," I said, in defence.

"No, Yunus! You are a Muslim and everything is from Allah! But, Yunus – listen to me *very* carefully – if you are *not* a Muslim anymore, it is punishable by death!"

It was true, I was not a Muslim anymore, but his words frightened me.

"I *am* a Muslim, *Alhamdulillah*!" I said, praising God, but I was lying. I said it out of fear and hung up the phone.

At night time I began to feel that someone was watching me. The full moon shone brightly, casting its cold light upon me, and it made me conspicuous. I looked out towards the surrounding hills flooded in the silvery light, and I felt vulnerable. In the middle of the night I awoke to the sound of footsteps coming towards me in my Sukkah-Tent and I froze with fear, but it was the footsteps of a gazelle walking on a path of volcanic stones.

As winter approached, the weather was wet and cold up in the hills. I covered my Sukkah-Tent with plastic sheeting, and to keep warm I lit a fire inside the Sukkah-Tent but choked on the smoke fumes. The plastic sheeting filled up with rainwater and burst, flooding my Sukkah-Tent, and in the morning I found myself sleeping in a pool of water.

In the daytime I wore all the clothing that I possessed, and at nighttime I slept in the same clothes. It was too cold to shower, and I gradually acquired a scruffy appearance — with a strong smell of sweat and smoke. My peaceful existence turned into loneliness, and the loneliness turned into a feeling of abandonment.

But then a black angel appeared; a night visitant who came to my Sukkah-Tent. He was a mystery to me, appearing out of nowhere, deep blue in colour and as dark as the night. My visitor was a German-Shepherd dog who came to keep me company when I was feeling lonely. He brought with him affection, and he slept in my Sukkah-Tent every night, guarding me until the morning when he disappeared — but always to return at nighttime.

Until one night when he did not return and I never saw him again.

I was sad to lose my friend, and I missed him a lot. But then I saw myself for what I had become: I was incapable of friendship with other human-beings, and I had become like a stray dog myself.

From that low place came the yearning rise up and live in the real world again.

I washed my clothes and hung everything out to dry in the sun, and showered and shaved. The next morning I got dressed into my clean clothes and headed straight to my psychiatrist in Jerusalem.

However, he used the same mantra: "No apartment: no therapy."

Once again I ended up in the Talbieh Psychiatric Hospital, but this time the duty doctor, a polite Arab man, listened to my story and said that he would help me. He brought me food to eat, and after a good night's sleep in the hospital, he arranged for me to see the head psychiatrist. I was told to leave my psychiatrist and was referred to the Talbieh Mental Health Rehabilitation Centre in Jerusalem.

I made regular visits to my new psychiatrist, a young and petite lady who wore her dark hair in a short tomboy cut, and she assigned me a competent therapist. She chose not to put me on medication, maintaining that it would slow down the process of therapy. She emphasized, however, that I was under no pressure of time while in treatment with them.

The major part of my treatment was the intensive psychotherapy with the assigned therapist. He was a likeable chap who had a large bulbous nose, and came to the clinic wearing hand-knitted sweaters, jeans and sandals. In the framework of treatment, part of my therapist's aim was to get me recognized by the Israeli National Insurance so that I would have rights and a disability income to live on. This involved a process of interviews and medical committees but eventually I was recognized as *disabled*.

My therapist then proceeded to arrange social housing, but in the meantime I hitchhiked from my Sukkah-Tent to Jerusalem for treatment. My therapist did not object to me living in my Sukkah-Tent, but it was the time of the second Palestinian Intifada uprising and there had been a number of violent attacks on Israeli civilians. I was completely alone in the hills, in my Sukkah-Tent, in the West Bank, and I was an easy target.

In the meantime, and as a precaution so as not to be too conspicuous, I lit my fire by daylight so that I could eat before sunset. Even so, a resident of Kfar Adumim, the nearby Jewish village, saw my Sukkah-Tent and came to tell me that I was in danger. He informed me that one of the two girls murdered in Wadi Kelt was from his village, and she was buried in a cemetery overlooking the hills where I lived. He was concerned that, if I was attacked, I would have absolutely no way to defend myself against a murderer. Therefore, he gave me his gun. I kept it loaded at all times and slept with it under my pillow at night.

Finally, after years of living outside, I received a letter stating that I had been approved housing.

I tied up the coarse hessian sacks to my Sukkah-Tent for the last time and paused to take one final look. My Sukkah-Tent had been my home for years, but so had the outside life, the surrounding hills, the sun by day, and the moon and stars by night: *they* were my home. I wondered what life would have in store for me next.

With a rucksack on my back and a fluttering of the heart, I walked down to the highway and waited for the bus to Jerusalem.

Chapter 25
Beit Shemesh

From the Central Bus Station in Jerusalem I took a bus to Beit Shemesh, a city in central Israel near the Valley of Elah, where I had been assigned government housing. I had mixed feelings: I feared the unknown, but I was excited at the prospect of living a new life in the real world.

I alighted from the bus in the heat of the day outside the offices of the state-owned housing company. With butterflies in my stomach, I walked up the stairs and introduced myself to the clerk. He had been expecting me and, with what seemed like a smirk on his face, he handed me the key.

I then proceeded to walk to the apartment building on Hamishlat Street. I passed rows of neglected, cheap quality building projects, which had been built in the 1950s to house North African immigrants who had previously lived in local refugee camps. It was on Hamishlat Street that the first permanent houses were built in the new town of Beit Shemesh; however, the buildings had become slums and now housed Israel's lowlife.

Somewhat cautiously I climbed the narrow, stifling-hot, stairwell to get to my assigned apartment. The cracked concrete walls, supported by heavy steel girders, were grubby and the stairs were black with grime. I reached the fourth floor, and upon opening the door to my apartment a flight of cooing pigeons swooped down on me. I was reminded of the Alfred Hitchcock horror film *The Birds*.

The apartment floor was thick with pigeon droppings from where they had perched and made their nests on the doors and windowsills. As I crept upon the slimy muck in an attempt to inspect the place, I had to stoop to avoid the birds as they flew frantically through the apartment. The apartment had become home to hundreds of pigeons.

Everything inside the apartment was broken. The kitchen unit was rotting, the marble countertop was on the floor, the sinks in the bathroom were smashed, the toilet bowl was cracked and black, and the windows were shattered over the floor. It was a depressing sight indeed, but I knew that if I would tell anyone about the condition of the apartment, they would never believe me! Therefore, I ran to the local photography shop and purchased a disposable camera. I photographed the interior of the apartment, and then I returned to the office of the state-owned housing company.

"Well?" said the clerk, grinning.

"Are you not ashamed to give me an apartment in such terrible condition?" I asked.

"Take it or leave it," said the clerk, abruptly.

That evening I went to stay with my religious friends in Gush Etzion, and there I wrote a letter to the Ministry of Housing. I enclosed the photographs and took it personally to the ministry the following morning. Thanks to the photographs, a week later I moved into the apartment while the workers were renovating it!

It was the month of July and the apartment, situated on the top floor, was extremely hot. The sun beat down on the tarred rooftop and made it feel like a furnace inside. The transformation from living in the Sukkah-Tent was a challenge; I had been accustomed to the outside life and was not yet psychologically ready to make the change. I made Bedouin tea on a camping stove, and I sat on the stone floor, next to the camping stove. I even planned to build a tent in my apartment.

After living outside for so long, I was suddenly conscious of how easy it was to cook without having to collect wood to make a fire. I realised how lucky I was to be able to take a shower without having to bring the water — and without having to heat it up first. I became aware of how easy it was to have light by simply pressing a switch. And yet, I did not want all these amenities and material comforts. I craved for the outside life, and I missed the sun and the moon and the stars. Therefore, I decided not to use electric lights and went to bed at nightfall and rose at dawn.

The workers doing the renovations saw me as a rare bird, but they were cordial and seemed to enjoy the prospect of drinking sweet Bedouin tea — made on my gas camping stove. From what I gathered, it was not at all unusual to have the odd character live in these buildings. However, they warned me that many of my neighbours were dangerous criminals, and they informed me there were drug dealers, alcoholics, whores and petty thieves in my building, and they advised me to avoid them at all costs.

When the engineer from the housing company came to see how the workers in my apartment were progressing, he immediately approved a new steel front-door with a multi-bolt locking mechanism.

"You will not be safe in this neighbourhood," he warned me; "you must put bars on all your windows."

When the telephone technician came to install a new telephone line, he said with a chuckle: "You're English and white, but you are living in Harlem!"

My neighbours, the children of North African immigrants, of whom the majority were from Morocco, took an immediate disliking to me. I had done nothing to harm them except that I was an Englishman, which they saw as a threat. They named me *The Maniac from London*.

They were traditional Jews who made an ostentatious display of religious observance, but at the same time they were dealing in drugs. The men wore *yarmulkes* and truly believed that they were righteous, when in fact they were extremely unpleasant criminals who made me cringe when I set eyes upon them. Occasionally they tried to provoke me, and when passing I could hear them uttering words of contempt. I shuddered with fear but knew that I had to be careful not to cross them, and I never answered back. They were unattractive, vulgar characters that reminded of the evolution of man and the great apes.

On the Sabbath the men had the habit of eating sunflower seeds, instead of smoking cigarettes which was forbidden on the Sabbath; they kept the sunflower seeds in their trouser pockets and their arms moved mechanically from pocket to mouth, continually swinging back and forth like a pendulum. Their mouths were constantly working, cracking the shells between their teeth and spitting them out: crack, eat, and spit; crack, eat, and spit.

The wives of these men were not feminine but were manipulative, hard women. I recall the phrase *mutton dressed up as lamb* which is exactly how I would describe the women in Beit Shemesh. All of the women had bleached blond hair, coarse facial features, and they used foundation make-up like putty for filling the holes and cracks. Their false finger nails, stuck onto stubby little fingers, had ready-painted art-designs, and the fingers were adorned with golden rings. Most of them were so overweight that they could not walk, but they waddled with their large bodies tilting from side to side while using their arms as paddles to propel themselves along.

The young girls were slim enough but by the age of sixteen they already had large buttocks due to a diet of fried dough. Like their mothers, they suffered from diabetes and other illnesses.

Large families and relatives gathered in the small 430-square-foot apartments, leaving the front doors open, apparently a sign of Israeli hospitality. They had loud discussions in the stairwell, for they did not know how to talk in a quiet and decent manner, and it occurred to me that it was a strange desire of theirs to be heard. The women sat on the stairs smoking cigarettes, the cigarette smoke sucked its way up into my apartment, and their loud, coarse sounding voices — speaking guttural Hebrew with a Moroccan dialect — echoed throughout the building. They had no consideration for others, except for their own clan, but occasionally accounts were settled in mafia style even within their own clan. On many an occasion I woke up in the middle of the night to the sight of torched cars outside my bedroom window.

The population was made up of mainly Jewish single mothers who had children from various men, some of whom were Arab men. The mothers lived in these small one-bedroom apartments with their children, and often with their latest boyfriends. The male children slept in the bedroom, and the girls slept in the living room with the mother, but also with the mother's latest boyfriend. The children were raised in a vicious circle of crime and abuse. They mixed with the same criminal types that hung around the building, and a neighbour's eight-year-old daughter was raped and murdered by one of them.

When I told friends in the UK about the types of people I lived with in Israel, they were astounded and asked, "Are you sure they are *Jews*?"

Eventually I yielded to my situation and brought my possessions out of storage. It had been years since I left Moshav Givat Yeshayahu for Wadi Kelt. Now I created a sanctuary in Beit Shemesh where I could detach myself from my neighbours. However, their loud voices still seeped into my apartment. I used earplugs to escape the noise, and nd to escape the unbearable heat on the top floor, I went for long walks.

On my walks I discovered more rows of cheaply built apartment buildings, some covered in a façade of Jerusalem-stone, that were supposedly of a better standard than where I lived — but the people were the same. They sat outside watching the traffic go by with blank expressions on their faces, seemingly unaware of the clouds of pollution that hung above them in the hot and still air. Laundry was hung over the railings and on portable laundry racks assembled on the public pavement. Obese women sat on garden chairs at the entrance to the buildings, some of them used mechanical fans with rattling propellers directed towards their open, plump legs, and the men sat on the walls drinking beer and vodka, whilst holding onto their large stomachs. Apparently these were the Children of Israel.

I had the use of my friend's car, but my downstairs criminal neighbour was envious and broke the locks, smashed the doors, and stole the spare wheel. I sued him in court but the other neighbours warned me that he would break my arms and legs in revenge. It turned out that he had nineteen claims pending in court and yet he was living the good life. Israel, it seemed, was a paradise for criminals.

I detested the world that I lived in and desperately wanted to leave Beit Shemesh, but I was trapped. There was no way out except suicide. But when I heard that a Russian born neighbour was found in an advanced stage of decomposition by the stench that came from his apartment, suicide was not an option anymore. The neighbours broke into his apartment and fought over his television set. I could not bear the thought of these people entering my apartment and stealing my possessions, even after I was dead.

My neighbours entered my life like parasites. They knocked on the door at all hours of the day to borrow things, and upon entering they would inform me of what furniture they would like — if I ever want to part with it. They asked the cost of every item in my apartment and repeatedly came to borrow, but they never returned a thing.

The downstairs criminal neighbour sent his wife and children away and married the mistress he was keeping on the side. He brought her and their son to replace his first wife and children, and it astonished me to see how the new wife was filled with pride. Shortly afterwards, I received a letter of apology from him over the car damage, stating that he had atoned for his sins, and asking me to withdraw my summons. I withdrew the summons but then she came knocking on my door to borrow things— and never returned them.

I meditated each morning to detach myself from my surroundings and the ugly world of Beit Shemesh. After a while my criminal neighbour (the one who had atoned for his sins) disappeared; his new wife confessed that he was in jail for a serious crime and would not return for many years.

Besides the local criminals, there were also Russian and Ethiopian immigrants who lived in the building. In an effort to make our entrance a little more pleasant, I washed the stairs and collected the money to pay for the stairwell lighting. One evening I knocked on the door of an elderly couple who were Russian immigrants and who did not speak Hebrew. For some reason the lady had the habit of speaking to me in Italian. On this particular occasion, she opened the door and stood completely naked in front of me, and my eyes nearly popped out of their sockets. Her frail and ashen body was as if it had risen from the dead; her long grey hair fell upon wilting breasts and her bony rib cage. In a trembling voice, I asked her for the money. She turned to bring small change, but then I noticed her husband lying on a divan, quite naked himself. As she handed me the coins she sang an aria from Verdi's *La Traviata*, after which she bowed her head graciously and closed the door.

Summer was stifling hot in Beit Shemesh and at night I lay naked on my bed with the windows wide open. The smell of cowsheds from Kibbutz Tzora drifted by in the sultry night, and the hint of cow dung triggered memories of my life on Kibbutz Ein

Gev. In the mornings I gazed out of my bedroom window, over the red roof-tops and the thousands of solar water heaters, towards the hills beyond. I had a view of the *moshavim* and *kibbutzim*, and in the valley below me, the train whistled on its journey from Tel Aviv to Jerusalem.

I decided to explore the areas around Beit Shemesh and started to take hikes. I visited the cowsheds in Kibbutz Tzora, and when hiking through the hills I came upon the Deir Rafat Monastery. The monastery had an imposing statue of the Virgin Mary that stood high against the blue sky, and around the monastery were ploughed fields with the sweet smell of freshly cut wheat.

I entered the monastery and sat down on the old, dark wooden pew and the rickety sound echoed throughout the chapel. I gazed up at the mural of angels painted on the ceiling; the words *Ave Maria* were painted in various languages on ribbons surrounding the angels, and a sister switched on her cassette-player with a recording of *Ave Maria*.

Outside of the monastery, I looked out over the vast green lowlands and descended the steep hill to explore the area. I wandered through the hills, past Bedouin encampments, and came to a rock where I sat and admired the view. The farmlands, belonging to the farming villages in the *Shephelah* lowlands, were sunlit in vivid colours of greens, yellows and the rich browns of freshly ploughed earth. The view reminded me of the British artist John Nash. The vibrant colours of never-ending fields faded into the distant horizon becoming neutral greys and my heart was filled with song. I sat staring into the landscape, and I seemed to transcend to a higher spiritual place somewhere beyond.

I lost all track of time while I was there, but as the sun began to go down I remembered that I have to return to my apartment – to my reality. But I asked myself, "What is reality?" I wondered why I let my unpleasant existence in Beit Shemesh be my reality when the places that surround Beit Shemesh could be my reality. I wandered back through the hills, feeling nature's miraculous healing, and stopped along the way to admire the wild flowers. As I climbed up the hill, the setting sun tinted the tall, wild grass a colour of copper, and the grass bowed down to me in the soft evening breeze.

I hitchhiked home, but as I walked towards my apartment I saw that there was a commotion in my neighbourhood. As I came closer I saw police cars, ambulances and the fire brigade. There was a huge crowd outside of my apartment building, and all the people there were looking up to *my* apartment.

I was stricken by fear and staggered towards the crowd.

"Here he is!" they all declared in harmony.

Everyone's eyes were on *me*, but I could not understand why. Then a police officer put his massive hand on my shoulder and led me away.

"What have I done?" I pleaded to know.

He said nothing.

Frightening thoughts filled my head; I pictured myself being handcuffed and deported from Israel. I felt nauseated as the police officer led me up the stairs to my apartment and I saw that my front door was open. The security bars on my windows had been cut, a window was smashed, and the firemen were walking over the broken glass. All my cupboards were open, and when I saw that my personal documents were overturned it became clear to me that they were searching for evidence.

The police officer told everyone to wait outside and sat me down on the sofa to talk. I trembled with fear, wondering whether I would be allowed to make one telephone call, for I had already decided that I would call my ex-therapist so that he could inform the police officer that I was not a traitor.

"You wrote a suicide note," the police officer said.

"*What?*"

I was completely dumbfounded by his statement.

But then I recalled that I had written some poetry early that morning and had sent it to some friends. I often wrote poetry to express my feelings, but apparently someone had tried calling me and there was no reply — because I had turned off my mobile phone while meditating in nature. That person called the police to inform them that I was committing suicide in my apartment. I broke down sobbing but the police officer comforted me. He brought me a glass of water and asked to see the email that I had sent. He read it and agreed that it was not a suicide note.

When I walked around Beit Shemesh I asked myself, "What am I doing here?" I despised Beit Shemesh and the people, but judging from the way that people stared at me, they seemed to despise me too! I must have seemed peculiar to them because I purposely tried to avoid eye contact.

I had become a loner, avoiding people, and yet it was not entirely out of choice. I could not relate to the people and saw the city as a reflection of the people; the place was filthy dirty, the buildings were shoddily built, and there was absolutely no beauty to be found. The city and the people depressed me so much that I asked the housing company a number of times for a transfer, but they would not approve my request.

On one of my hikes into nature, I walked far out into the hills that surround Beit Shemesh and discovered Wadi Dolev, a valley filled with pasture lands. As I walked through the *wadi*, thousands of dark-blue eyes peered out at me from fields of wild poppies, their little faces blushing scarlet red as I passed by. I inhaled a sweet perfume as my sandals cut through the blades of luscious green grass, but then the brown pellets of droppings, fresh under the soles of my sandals, informed me that there was a herd grazing in the vicinity. I came upon a large Bedouin tent with the aroma of cooking fires and burning wood.

Wadi Dolev is an area to where Bedouins from the Negev Desert come north to graze their flocks. Fond memories of my Bedouin family in Wadi Kelt came back as I watched in admiration a lone shepherd with his flock of sheep. As I approached the shepherd boy, I sensed the strong odour of sweat and livestock which for me represented nature and naivety, purity and authenticity. I spoke with the wild looking boy and was seized by a need to be part of his world, but I realised that I was a lost soul searching for love and a place to belong.

I continued on my way, climbing the hills, and came to a pine forest planted by the Jewish National Fund. Inside the forest I found an abandoned village, hidden by the forest. I was mystified by what I had found and an eerie feeling gripped me, but I continued walking on. I passed some old houses with crumbling walls, and there were almond trees in full blossom in an abandoned garden, and then a mosque and a well.

And then I stopped dead in my tracks. A light was projecting directly onto the scene, giving it a dramatic effect. I looked up at the tall pine-trees, up towards the sun's rays that filtered through, and realised that it was showing me a world where people had once lived but now lay in ruins, and yet the pink almond blossom was still very much alive.

With a heavy heart I walked on, past fig trees and carob trees, and past a *moshav* built on the village grounds. I was convinced that I had discovered a great secret, but to my surprise I came across a tiny sign placed there by the Jewish National Fund. The sign read *Dayr Aban.* It was once an Arab village, but like many Arab villages that existed at the time, it had been abandoned by the Arabs during Israel's War of Independence in 1948.

That same evening my mobile-phone rang, and to my surprise a name from the past lit up on the screen. The call was from Ahmad, *mukhtar* of the Bedouin tribe in Jericho. The reason he called was to tell me that Atta's son Jabril had fallen down the cliff while shepherding in Wadi Kelt, and was assumed dead. However, an Israeli doctor hiking in the area inspected the body and discovered that Jabril was not dead. The doctor dialled 100 and a medical team from the Israeli Army came to attend to Jabril at the bottom of the ravine. Upon inspection, the medics organized a helicopter with a rescue team.

The helicopter with the rescue team hovered above the medics in the canyon and lowered a line with a rescue stretcher. The medics taped Jabril onto the rescue stretcher, and he was lifted out of the *wadi*, into the helicopter, and flown directly to Hadassah Hospital in Jerusalem.

Atta, however, lived in Wadi Kelt and was registered under the Palestinian Authority in Jericho. He had to arrange for an entry visa into Israel to visit his son Jabril at Hadassah Hospital. Ahmad had telephoned me to ask if I would go to the hospital to be with Jabril until his father got there. I was too tired after my hike and answered that Jabril was in good hands, and I would go first thing in the morning.

As I approached the hospital entrance the following morning, I felt a sense of guilt when I saw that Atta had already arrived. He was speaking on his mobile-phone at the entrance to the hospital and looked very distinguished in a mustard coloured *Gallabiyah*, a brown coloured cloak with gold edging, and a pin-striped turban. He had grown a full beard and shaved his moustache, as is the custom to follow in the ways of the Prophet Muhammad. Upon sighting me, he immediately closed his flip phone with a snap and greeted me with a kiss. As we hugged, I sensed a strong cigarette odour in his bushy beard. He looked at me with his beady eyes, and giggled in the same way that he always did, but he was a changed man.

"Atta, how is Jabril?" I inquired.

"Jabril is on a medical ventilator but *Alhamdulillah* he is alive," said Atta, and looking up to the skies he praised God once again, "*Alhamdulillah!*"

He told me that he had been sure that Jabril was dead, and how sad it made him feel.

"Atta, *Alhamdulillah*, but maybe you should be praising the Israeli Army instead?" I asked, with sarcasm.

"Yunus, I could not believe my eyes when they taped him onto a stretcher and took him up into the helicopter!"

"Atta, do you remember how Eid was angry with me for going to the Israeli Army, *to the enemy*, when I was attacked by Jasser in Wadi Kelt?"

He hung his head and pondered on my words, but said nothing.

Atta had become somewhat of a celebrity in the hospital, and was treated with respect having acquired the honourable title of *Sheikh*. The doctors and nurses referred to him as *Sheikh* Atta, even though he knew that he was not a sheikh. It amused me to see that he was enjoying this immensely.

After a while his cousin Rizik came to visit. Rizik was Eid's son, the younger brother of Mustafa, and now a married man with children. He was a good-looking fellow but skinny as a rake. He had light brown hair, smooth olive skin, and his features were sharp; the hollows of his eyes, his high cheek bones, and his chin were as if chiselled from stone, and his eyes were a stunning jade green.

I suggested that the three of us go for a walk as there was not a lot that we could do at the hospital, while Jabril was on a medical ventilator. We took a path that led to the picturesque village of Ein Kerem, a village surrounded by hills and forests. As we were walking, however, I realised that I was taking them to an abandoned Arab village – that had been resettled by Jews after 1948.

As we entered the village, with the ancient terraced slopes on one side, the Arab houses came into view; they were grand buildings built with exquisite architectural details of arched windows and wrought iron verandas. Between the buildings were quaint little alleyways paved in cobblestone.

According to Christian tradition Elizabeth, mother of John the Baptist, and Mary, mother of Jesus, met in Ein Kerem next to the village well, referred to as Mary's spring, but now it has a mosque built over it.

Upon seeing the mosque Rizik suddenly roared: "It's *ours*! Ein Kerem is *ours*!"

I was taken aback by the outburst and replied in a feeble voice: "But Rizik, the Arabs left Ein Kerem."

"*No* Yunus! The Jews killed the Arabs in the village of Deir Yassin, and the Arabs in Ein Kerem had to flee before they were massacred too!" he yelled.

People stopped to look at what all the commotion was about, but he was right. I could not argue with him for I knew that there were abandoned villages in Israel, and yet it was not that simple.

Although I was not an observant Jew, over the years I had taken on the identity of Jew again, but after meeting Atta and Rizik and being called by my Muslim name, I felt confused. I still felt part of my Bedouin family, and I missed them a lot.

We stopped outside of a *café* and I invited them in for a coffee but they refused to enter for fear that alcoholic beverages would be served there. Instead, we ordered carrot juice at a kiosk and I tried to get Rizik to see the good side of the Jews. I reminded him of how the Israeli Army had saved Jabril and of the good care he was receiving in Hadassah Hospital. But he would have none of it.

"Hadassah is *ours*!" he squealed.

This made me laugh.

"Rizik, Hadassah is an organization founded by Jews," I said.

"That's alright, Yunus; Jews can work for Muslims as *dhimmis*, but it's all ours!" he replied.

When we returned to Hadassah Hospital, Rizik and Atta went to wash and pray. I sat outside on a bench and waited, but my head began to pound with a severe migraine. I was sick and tired of the conflict, and I wished that I could run away to somewhere neutral. I wanted to find peace, to live on a farm with animals, or to live by the sea or by a river; I just wanted to be alone with nature. I closed my eyes to soothe the pain, and I imagined that I was living in a neutral land and saw myself fishing on the banks of a lake. In this imaginary world, I ran my hands through the soft and cool grass, and in the background I saw a lone cottage with window-boxes and blooms of scarlet geraniums. But then I wondered what would my name be in that neutral land? I could not have a Hebrew name or an Arabic name, but I would need a neutral name in a neutral land!

Rizik and Atta returned and sat on the bench to smoke a cigarette. They inhaled in silence, but Rizik announced that it was late and he would have to take the bus to Jerusalem from where he would transfer to East Jerusalem, and from there to Jericho by taxi on the Palestinian side.

I remained alone with Atta so that we could talk about his religious way of life and religious education in Yattah, near Hebron, where he was studying.

"Yunus, I highly recommend the Centre for Islamic Studies for you because there you will learn *pure* Islam, and not the Islam that Rizik talks about which is pure politics!"

I pondered over this, and valued his advice very much. I was tempted, but then he told me the following story:

"Yunus," he said, giggling. "The Imam says that the Jews are like dogs!"

I looked at him in disbelief.

"I'm serious, Yunus! The Imam said that dogs give birth to maybe eight or nine puppies at a time, but you don't see so many dogs around."

I looked at him blankly.

"The Jews are the same," he said. "They have been around for thousands of years but how many Jews do you see?" He had some difficulty controlling his giggle, but quickly composed himself. "Yunus," he said in a low and serious tone: "How many Jews are there in the world and how many Muslims?"

*

Epilogue

My religious experience in Israel as a Jew and as a Muslim made a huge impact on my spiritual life. I believe in God, meaning that I believe in a single and invisible Deity that is in control of this world, but I am not affiliated with any religion. I pray in self-seclusion, and I pray to God in my own words. And yet I choose to lay *Tefillin*, and I recite the *Shema Yisrael*, because I feel that this is what God wants of me.

I believe that Judaism is a way of life created by a learned and intelligent people who believed that it was the way of life that God desired. I have no doubt that God communicated His will through them. The Hebrew Bible, however, is written in the language of men; it can only be their interpretation and indeed an interpretation of a people influenced by the environment that they lived in at the time. God's message came from a higher spiritual realm, but not in the human language. My point being, the Hebrew Bible is a compilation of sacred literature written over a period of time by Jews. Not by God.

How ironic then that the Qur'an contains references to events in the Hebrew Bible, and that Muslims consider the Qur'an to be the word of God!

I have forgiven Jasser for his attack on me because I believe that it was the hand of God that took me out of Wadi Kelt. I visited him and his family, but as far as the Bedouins in the West Bank are concerned, for me to be anything other than a Muslim is punishable by death. I therefore had to pretend that I was a religious Muslim. I came to the conclusion that I was fooling myself in thinking that I could have lived in a society like theirs; I was caught up in a world of hope and make-believe.

It has been twenty years since I tied up the hessian sacks to my Sukkah-Tent and came to live in Beit Shemesh. My experiences in Beit Shemesh were written in the past tense, but nothing has changed; they should have been written in the present tense! I still live with the same neighbours, but my apartment has become my haven, a place for me to exist safely in my own world, detached from the people.

But this is not the life that I want. I want to detach myself from society altogether, and to live in the wilderness, on the shores of a lake or a river, in a cave or in a hut. I love the Land of Israel, the mountains and the desert, and want to live close to the earth. I love nature and animals, but not people.

This book is about my *Israel* experience, but there is more to me than that. I had a mental breakdown in Israel perhaps because I came to Israel with a past, but in Israel you are forced to identify by your religion, and religion in Israel is who you are: it's your identity. I often ask myself, "Who am I?" and whether I belong in Israel. I cannot help wondering how my life would have been if I did not come to Israel, and had remained John Robert Screeton.

I am now writing three novels about one soul. My first novel is now published:

YUNUS – a novel, by Yonatan Shaked.

***

My Sukkah-Tent on the grounds of an abandoned nursery.

Printed in Great Britain
by Amazon